THE BEST OF

Vance Havner

THE BEST OF

BAKER BOOK HOUSE
Grand Rapids, Michigan

Trade edition first published March 1988

ISBN: 0-8010-4326-3

Sixth printing, March 1992

Printed in the United States of America

CONTENTS

PREFACE

I AM HAPPY to write an introductory word for this volume
of selections from my devotionals and sermons of the past
thirty years. Here is a cross-section of my messages from
the days of a country pastorate to the stepped-up pace
of the late 60's. The tempo has quickened but I hope
that what is recorded here is of the truth unchanged
and unchanging. We began these meditations strolling
beside still waters and now we write sometimes aboard
a jet. We hope that the discord of these days has not
thrown any of the notes off-key.

This little book also bridges thirty years of pleasant
association with the same publisher and offers a sampling
of the material that has brought precious letters from
friends around the world. Many of these friends we have not
seen but all belong to a blessed fellowship by reason of
what we share in common.

Paperbacks often go where other books are not found
and it is hoped that these reflections clad in plainer garb
may be a blessing where costlier tomes might not be read.
The author anticipates his first paperback and welcomes
a new circle of readers.

VANCE HAVNER

JOURNEY FROM JUGTOWN

WHEN ABRAHAM'S SERVANT started out to look for a wife
for Isaac, he prayed for divine guidance. He needed it.
A man looking for a wife for himself needs all the light
he can get. This man was looking for a wife for somebody
else! Later on he said, *"I being in the way, the Lord
led me . . ."* (GENESIS 24:27).

This is my testimony from the summit of the years.
I would change that little chorus a bit and sing, "My
Lord led the way through the wilderness; all I had to
do was to follow."

I grew up in the North Carolina hills. From our front
porch we could see at night the lights of five little towns.
From the back porch one could see Grandfather Mountain, Table Rock, and companion peaks standing like sen-
tinels along the western skyline. My home community was
called Jugtown because in the early years there were little
shops up and down the road where potters wrought vessels
of clay. I lived the simple, happy life of an old-fashioned
country boy. I tramped the woods with a shepherd dog.
There was plenty of outdoors, and all the plain joys of
rustic youth uncushioned by modern conveniences. It
would drive a teen-ager frantic these days but I thrived
on it.

Father was an austere but devout Christian, the pastor's
right-hand man at old Corinth Baptist Church. The country preachers always stayed at our house on Saturday

before the fourth Sunday in each month, when they came by horse and buggy to preach the monthly sermon. Some of those sermons were long enough to last a month and sounded more like filibusters—but it was sound preaching. Father always let me sit up late on those Saturday nights, before the open fire, and listen to him and the minister talk about the things of God. It beat all the television that has been seen since.

Father should have been a preacher. Two of his brothers did preach; one as a Baptist, the other as a Methodist. Mother was a gentle, kindly soul content to be a housewife. Her life as a "keeper at home" would be anathema to the emancipated woman of today.

I grew up with a Bible in one hand and a bird book in the other. *Pilgrim's Progress, Foxe's Book of Martyrs,* and a set of good classical literature formed our library. I never knew the day when I did not feel that I should preach and write. I memorized Bible portions, made little Sunday School talks, and sent my first "sermon" to our small-town newspaper when I was nine.

When I was ten, I professed faith in Christ. A revival was in progress at Corinth Church, but I came to Jesus alone in the woods. Always following an unbeaten path, I did not go to the mourner's bench as the custom was, but made my decision in a solitary place. There was no dramatic experience such as some can relate; I came as a child in simple trust. I did not understand all about the plan of salvation. I do not understand all about electricity, but I don't intend to sit in the dark until I do.

I was baptized in the South Fork River and a year later I asked the church to license me to preach. I began with a talk at the First Baptist Church of Hickory, twelve miles from my home. I have been in bigger towns and churches since, but none looked as large as did Hickory that night. Dad and I went over in an early Ford with thirty horsepower—twenty of them dead. I stood on a chair and spoke while the pastor of the church stood on one side and the state evangelist stood on the other: like Aaron and Hur holding up the hands of Moses.

For several years I preached on Sundays in town and country churches as a boy preacher. Of course, crowds came out of curiosity. Then I went to a Baptist boarding school called South Fork Institute. I was not a star student, but often sat listening to a bird singing outside rather than to a professor teaching on the inside. I went next to what is now Gardner-Webb College. It was during the First World War. We were singing *Tipperary* and *Over There,* and girl students wept as boy friends left for camp and for France to make the world safe for democracy. It hasn't been safe for anything since.

The principal of this school advised me, one day, to blaze my own trail instead of following the prescribed course of ministerial training. He told me that I was no genius, but would do well to follow an unbeaten path. I went on to Catawba College for a year, then to Wake Forest. I was restless and wanted to preach. One day, I packed my belongings and left. A professor saw me at the railroad station and said, "Young man, you'll regret this." I haven't regretted it yet. I am not advising others to follow that course, but I believe it was best for me.

I started preaching again, but without guidelines or precedent for my kind of ministry. I made many mistakes, went up blind alleys and dead-end streets. I took a rural pastorate in eastern North Carolina. I became somewhat enamored of the liberal approach which was beginning to gain favor. It did not become malignant in my case, but I did have enough of the virus in my system to preach popular sermons that convicted nobody. The unbelievers liked my preaching and I had a good crowd, but many of them died unsaved under my ministry.

I resigned after one year and returned to my old home in the hills. Father died that winter, leaving mother and me with a grocery store which was robbed and burned one night. The Lord made it clear to my heart that if

I would preach the old message I had proclaimed as a boy, He would make a way for me. I remember reading J. Gresham Machen's *Christianity and Liberalism* out in the woods to my great profit. I returned to the old message, and the first thing I had to do was go back to my country pastorate and preach it for three years. I studied my Bible, tramped the country roads, and laid a good foundation for the years to come. No preacher has had complete preparation who has not been pastor of a country church. It still affords, even in this insane age, some opportunity for meditation and reflection in solitude, that lost art of the modern ministry.

From 1934 to 1939, I was pastor of the oldest Baptist Church in the South, the First Church of Charleston, S. C. I shall always treasure those five years in that quaint, historic old city. Many blessed experiences were mine, especially a stirring of my heart as to the filling of the Holy Spirit. I was brought to a new dimension by reading *Deeper Experiences of Famous Christians*.

In my country pastorate, I had written my first book, *By the Still Waters*. I wrote for the *Charlotte Observer* and for religious publications. One of them, *Revelation,* edited by Donald Grey Barnhouse of Philadelphia, was helpful in opening doors up north for Bible Conferences. Moody Bible Institute's Founder's Week, Winona Lake, Montrose, Maranatha, Pinebrook, Canadian Keswick, and on the West Coast, the Torrey Conference in Los Angeles, Mount Hermon and the Firs—these, and many more, eventually appeared on my itinerary. "I being in the way, the Lord led me." No man with God's message need politick, nor pull wires, nor sit hunched over cafeteria tables making contacts, nor wait for some talent scout to find him. He need not chase key men around, if he knows the Keeper of the keys!

So many calls came that I left Charleston and took to the road in 1940. I was in a low state physically, for I had been suffering from nervous exhaustion for two years, and a traveling ministry seemed the last thing a preacher in my condition should undertake. It meant getting adjusted and yet never getting adjusted week after week to different beds, food, climates, environment, and continually rising to the occasion. Yet the way had opened, and I could only go forward.

My first engagement was with the Mel Trotter Mission Bible Conference in Grand Rapids. I got as far as Chicago, came down with the flu, and wound up in a hospital. The devil sat on the foot of the bed and laughed at my discomfiture. The doctor told me to go south. I wired the Florida Bible Institute and accepted an invitation I had declined earlier. There I recuperated, and met the gracious little lady who became my wife and has meant more to me than anyone else on earth. The Lord knew I needed to go south instead of north! Also, in that school I met a lean, lanky student by the name of Billy Graham. We had our pictures taken on the campus. Twenty years later, we posed for another snapshot. What God wrought in twenty years!

I married Sara Allred in 1940, and we took to the road. I could write a book on how the Lord has made a way for us without any conniving on my part. I have seen doors open that I couldn't have pried loose with a crowbar. I have no organization and have never prepared even a brochure for publicity, yet I could have kept another man busy with calls I could not accept. Satan tried to tell me that nobody would stand for my kind of preaching, and that I would starve to death. I look like I'm starving, but I eat three meals a day. I am often reminded of Will Rogers. During the depression of the thirties, when college graduates were walking the streets looking for work, Will was making a good living in his homely way. One day he said to a friend, "It's dinner time and I ain't et." His friend suggested, "You mean you haven't eaten." Will replied, "I notice that a lot of people who haven't eaten *ain't et!*"

From Bible conferences all over the country, and from church revivals, I gradually became occupied almost full time with my own denomination, the Southern Baptists. I had been a Southern Baptist since I was a boy, except for a brief time when I was a member of First Baptist, Minneapolis, Minnesota, while Dr. W. B. Riley was pastor. Dr. Riley baptized my wife who had been of the Quaker persuasion. I was on a program with Dr. W. A. Criswell of First Baptist, Dallas, in a conference held in the old Baptist Tabernacle of Atlanta, Georgia. Later, I was invited to the Texas Evangelistic Conference for 1949, meeting in First Baptist Church of Dallas. Thus began a new field of ministry in evangelistic conferences, as well as church revivals, all over the convention.

A serious illness in 1960 almost took my life. After major surgery, a blood clot brought me to the door of death. A fine Christian nurse sat by my bed all that night, at her own request, praying and watching. Prayers went up all over the country from Moody Bible Institute to the Florida Baptist Evangelistic Conference where I was to have been speaking. Billy Graham called my wife that night from Miami to say, "We had prayer for Vance and I told my wife that I believed the Lord would let Vance live awhile longer to prepare sermons for the rest of us to preach!" The Lord definitely healed me, and after five months out of the pulpit, I started again in First Baptist of Houston, Texas.

Today, after twenty-seven years on the road, fifty-two years in the ministry, and twenty books, I can only marvel at the way God has gone before me in this journey from Jugtown. Abraham's servant, when he found the wife for Isaac, was invited to linger ten days, but he said, "Hinder me not, seeing the Lord hath prospered my way . . ." (GEN-ESIS 24:56). I am resolved to make that reply when any subtle suggestion arises to take it easy and relax on my heavenly errand. When God has prospered a man's way, he had better be on his way!

All the way my Saviour leads me.
What have I to ask beside?
Can I doubt His tender mercy
Who through life has been my Guide?

Retirement age is supposed to mean that I should sit in a rocking chair, wait for my social security check, and reminisce about the good old days. I have no thought of retiring. I would say with Caleb, " ... *give me this mountain ...*"*!* (JOSHUA 14:12). I am not asking for mole-hills. Old soldiers need not fade away. I have asked like Hezekiah for *an extension of time;* like Jabez, for *an enlargement of coast;* like Elisha, for *an endurement of power.* Caleb did not suffer, like the ten frightened spies, from a grasshopper complex. Too many cowards are cringing before the giants of Anak. God give us Calebs looking for mountains to conquer!

BIBLE WINDOW-SHOPPING

A FAMILIAR figure on the streets is the window-shopper who moves along gazing fondly in each show-window but buying nothing. In the realm of things spiritual we have with us the Bible window-shopper. He moves along through the Book reading its precious promises, hearing its high challenges, looking at its deep messages of peace and power and victory. But he never makes them his own. He appreciates but does not appropriate. He respects his Bible, argues for it, counts it dear, but its rich treasures never become living realities in his own experience. He is a window-shopper amongst the storehouses of God's revealed truth.

On the way, he passes by where is displayed such a choice jewel as *"We know that all things work together for good to them that love God, to them who are the called according to His purpose."* "What a rare pearl that is!" he exclaims. "What a lofty faith one needs to believe that!" So he moves on and the treasure stays on exhibition. He does not go in and claim it, though, if he be a believer, it is his and is there for him. He is only window-shopping.

How many believers loiter along the Bible stores and come away empty. *"My God shall supply all your need according to His riches in glory by Christ Jesus."* One reads that devoutly and, an hour later, is worrying about adversity and bemoaning his hard circumstances! *"They which receive abundance of grace and of the gift of right-eousness shall reign in life by One, Jesus Christ."* Another

16

looks at that gem and lives like a pauper when God meant him to be a prince. *"All things are yours,"* there are many who behold that free pass to all God's unlimited stock, yet live spiritually almost bankrupt. Window-shoppers!

The storehouse of God's Word was never meant for mere scrutiny, not even primarily for study but for sustenance. It is not simply a collection of fine proverbs and noble teachings for men to admire and quote as they might Shakespeare. It is rations for the soul, resources of and for the spirit, treasure for the inner man. Its goods exhibited upon every page are ours, and we have no business merely moving respectfully amongst them and coming away none the richer.

The window-shopper upon the streets often has a very good reason for not buying: he has not the wherewithal. But no believer can say that of God's riches, for the treasure of His Word is without money and without price. Whosoever will may drink freely. Some window-shop because they never have fully realized that the things of the Spirit can be made actual, living realities here and amidst this humdrum, daily round of commonplace duties. Others loaf along, indifferent to their inward poverty, faring scantily when the banquets of God are at their disposal. And some substitute wishful longing for the practical realization of the Christ-life.

The Lord is rich unto all who call upon Him. Let us have done with this idle window-shopping. Let us go into the deep stores of His Word, rummage among its treasurers new and old, and come forth from each excursion laden with the bounty in the Book.

A MORNING CONCERT

IT IS NOW officially spring-time. The wood-thrush has returned and stamped it with his approval. I heard him this
morning in an early recital. I stood beside a stretch of
calmest water unruffled by even the faintest breeze. Beyond
rose the deep woods and from the edge of the moss-hung
cypresses the clear call of the feathered flutist was borne
across the little lake to me.

It was a perfect setting and the serene singer was at
his best. There is something about such moments, the holy
quietness, the cadences of that woodland voice, the tonic
freshness of springtime, that sets one's soul longing for
a world untainted by sordidness and sin. One catches a
passing glimpse of what this earth once was like before
the blight of death and corruption and yearns to escape
from the absurd nightmare of modernity to some restful
haven where the delirium tremens of "progress" has not
come.

Nearby where I stood baby-ducks paddled in the water.
High overhead I caught the note of passing wild geese
and looked in time to see them, faintly visible, a happy
brigade homeward bound. On all sides arose the tumult
of new voices, the cardinal, the water thrush, the yellow-
throat, the vireo, the warblers. In a world even as broken
and bruised as it is today, there are many reminders of
a blessed harmony still to come. These intruders of loveli-

18

ness are not tantalizing jests of an ironical fate, brighter moments of a maniac universe bound for oblivion. Paradise shall be restored!

The wood-thrush has begun again. The best part of his song escapes when one tries to set it down in words, but there is an elusive something in the lilt of those tones that brings back memories of carefree days long passed. A ragged country youngster who stayed in the woods with his shepherd dog; high dreams of youth and lofty visions; happy summer days in sylvan solitudes, the woods his fairyland, bird and butterfly his elves and sprites. Hard reality and the stern necessities of this artificial age have toned down the calliope notes of youth, but in such rare moments we escape the modern grind while the wood-thrush turns backward old Time in his flight.

But in these later years we have learned to rejoice in a blessed truth of the Book. We cannot believe that the loveliness of Nature is doomed to extinction. We believe that *"the whole creation groaneth and travaileth in pain together until now,"* waiting *"for the manifestation of the sons of God."* As man sings amid his troubles in hope of a better world we like to think the song of the wood-thrush is an expression of a longing creation yearning for a redeemed earth. Instead of losing our hope for a land of pure delight in the midst of this matter-minded world, we grow daily more confident of reaching through our Lord the new Paradise, where *"the wolf also shall dwell with the lamb."*

How tragic that men have so lost themselves in the modern scramble for a life that consisteth in the abundance of the things one possesseth that these imitations of a better world fall on ears utterly deafened! How many ever hear the message of the wood-thrush? If ever they go to the woods it is to slay and kill. If they hear a bird it is a caged canary! No wonder we have grown so dry and destitute.

Shut off your radio and attend a woodland concert. Deep will call unto deep, and if you listen in the light of His Word you shall hear things high and holy.

GOD'S POST-OFFICE

OUR POST-OFFICE is a dull and commonplace affair, viewed from without by the uninterested passer-by. One would hardly connect it with anything thrilling or romantic. Just a little wired cage, a few boxes, a desk and a table—can anything worth while come through that little window from such a plain and unpoetic corner of a country store?

Indeed there can! Through that little window have come messages that have sent me fairly skipping down the road, gleeful as a farm-boy on his first spring fishing trip. It has relayed to me letters which have fairly changed the course of my career. And from that very ordinary post-office have come missives that have saddened my soul.

Really there are few places on earth more charged with human interest than a post-office. Have you ever thought how packed with joy and sorrow, despair and delight, one ugly mail-bag may be? Have you reflected how one day's batch of letters may file out through that little window to prosper some and pauperize others, lead this man to marriage and that to murder, kill here and cure there? I've almost decided our little old post-office is the most romantic place of all!

But the post-office is not a source, it is only a medium. It does not create these potent messages, it only relays them from the creator to you. You and I are human post-offices. We are daily giving out messages of some sort to the world. They do not come from us, but through us; we do not create, we convey. And they come either from hell or from heaven.

Men study how to make their lives more interesting. Take a lesson from the post-office. It is interesting, not because of itself, but because of what it passes on to men. The world will make a beaten path to your door if you bring them news from heaven. What letters go through the window of your life? Letters of truth and hope, to cheer and console? Or do you hand out dirty trash, worthless drivel, selfish commercial circulars, black-edged missives of misery?

Every Christian is a postmaster for God. His duty is to pass out good news from above. If the postmaster kept all the mail and refused to give it out, he would soon be in trouble. No wonder some Christians are so miserable: they keep God's blessing within their own little lives, and soon there is congestion. God does not send us good things from the heavenly headquarters merely for óur personal enjoyment. Some of them may be addressed to us, but most of them belong to our fellow-men, and we must pass them on.

He would be a poor postmaster who spent his time decorating the post-office and failed to distribute the mail. For people do not come there to see the post-office: they come for the mail. The Christian seriously misunderstands his work as God's postmaster if he spends his time decorating his place of business and neglect to deliver God's messages through him to men. To be sure, a clean and tidy post-office is desirable, and so is a holy life: but it is easy for one to become so engrossed in introspection that he make his goodness his business. Keeping our lives clean is only tidying up the office so we may carry on God's business. When it becomes an end in itself, nothing passes out to men.

How thrilling the plainest life can be when it becomes a function in God's great system and not a selfish enterprise! The tiniest post-office can bear a letter that may wreck or bless a nation. And the simplest life can relay blessings that may rock a continent toward God.

If you are a believer, you are God's postmaster in the little nook where you live. Keep the office clean, but do not make that more important than delivering the messages. Men will soon learn to gather at the window and will bring you, in return, letters of their own to pass on to others.

WHICH IS DESERT

*Arise and go toward the south unto the way . . . which
is desert. And he arose and went: and behold . . .*
(ACTS 8:26,27).

PHILIP IS IN the midst of a great revival in Samaria
when suddenly there comes a strange turn in the Divine
direction. I am sure friends must have said: "What! From
a revival to a desert? Are you sure God wants you to
leave these thrilling meetings for a desolate trail?" But
he went and behold . . . the evangelist meets the eunuch.

Has God called you from a Samaria to a Sahara? Has
health failed, has adversity shut down, have loved ones
gone, must you undertake a hard work among strangers?
Does the sudden shift in His orders seem so abrupt that
you hesitate and argue that it doesn't make sense? Ah,
but His ways are not ours. If He sends you to the desert
He can furnish streams of water there. Philip had a date
with the eunuch and didn't know it. If God orders you
out on the lone road He has a date for you to keep with
someone, maybe with some bewildered soul, maybe with
Himself. Jesus must needs go through Samaria to meet
one needy woman; perhaps you must needs leave Samaria
because somewhere out on a dismal way, not at all where
you like to travel, someone needs you.

Philip *"arose and went . . . and behold."* He Who has said, *"go ye therefore . . ."* has said *"lo, I am with you."* As you obey, you may not see the *why* of it, but you shall see the *Who*. He Who says "Go" goes along.

THE LADY IN THE KITCHEN

I CAN HEAR her back in the kitchen. There is an occasional rattle of pans and dishes. After awhile dinner will be ready and there will be a gracious presence to greet me as I go into eat things I like, fixed as I like them. After weeks on the road eating in one Public (Pto) Main(e) Dining Room after another, I get to where everything tastes alike. But several days at home restores me. For I found, a little late but "better late than never," that species of vanishing American, a good wife who can cook. Wives of yesterday could cook; now they just go to school and study cooking. Dietetics, home economics—you can't live on that.

I found more than that. An old-fashioned girl who made up her mind years ago not to follow the crowd, a Quaker, too, with all that normally means in conviction and character, from whose dictionary "duty" and "discipline" and "responsibility" had not been dropped. Nor do I want you to envision a drab figure in the clothes of yesterday. It takes something amounting almost to genius for a preacher's wife to go shopping for clothes and emerge later from her dressing-room looking like neither a dummy of the long ago in the Smithsonian Institution nor, on the other hand, a modernized resident of Sodom or Gomorrah. I say it takes something akin to genius, but the Lady in the Kitchen has it, and from the first new hat all done up with roses she has managed to crown her head with a smart top-piece that still looks like a hat.

The woman who marries a traveling preacher would do well to engage in a little extra praying. Marrying a preacher, whether stationary or peripatetic, puts any poor woman on the spot. She will be scrutinized far more than ever her spouse will be, and anything she says or does will be wrong to some people. Add to the trials that come any preacher's way the career of a rolling stone and a woman will think more than twice before she signs up for a life that courts acute indigestion by day and insomnia by night.

But the Lady in the Kitchen has done it. She has sat in church auditoriums all over America and listened incognito while her husband was being discussed around her. And she has picked up some gems, if you will believe me. Some things she has heard might have tempted me to pride but the Lord always provides something on the debit side to save my hatband from expansion. She has had personal workers try to get her up to the mourner's bench. She has been asked countless times what she thought of the visiting preacher. She has heard all her husband's stories and starts smiling 'way before I get to the smiling place.

She has done it all with good grace and I know the reason why. No amount of good nature or fortitude can equip anyone for such a mission. It is a divine calling and requires divine strength. More than one poor man has ventured into it with a woman who did it not as unto the Lord. Only friction and heartbreak can follow. No wonder Paul advised marriage only in the Lord. Paul did not "lead about a wife" as did Peter, but he sensed that just any woman cannot be so led about and come out smiling.

But the Lady in the Kitchen summons me. I'll go see "what's cooking."

FATHER'S SERMON

*Ye are our epistle written in our hearts, known and read
of all men . . . manifestly declared to be the epistle of
Christ . . .* (II CORINTHIANS 3:2, 3).

"A CHRISTIAN IS the world's Bible," said Moody, "and
some of them need revising." Don't forget that your life
is preaching the "Gospel according to you."

My father, a faithful layman who loved preaching and
preachers, used to tell us once in a while, with a smile:
"Some time I'm going to prepare a big sermon and preach
it." I think he really meant it for I found sermon notes,
beginnings of outlines which never were completed. Whether the task was too great or whether he was smitten with
timidity, I do not know, but for some reason the sermon
never materialized.

Some months after he passed away, I was preaching
in the old home church in the country. One night I asked
Christians to stand and tell who had led them to Christ.
I did not know what I was getting into: so many arose
and said, "It was your father who brought me to Jesus"
that I felt embarrassed lest the people think I had planned
it merely to honor my father. They told of how along
the country ways, in their homes, in the little church, he
had dealt with them for the Lord.

And then I knew: Father *had* preached his big sermon, after all!

PREACHER UNWANTED

THE PULPIT COMMITTEE was having no end of trouble considering pastoral candidates. All the prospects were too young or too old, not sociable or too sociable, too flashy or too drab, too this or too that. One day somebody remarked, "I was just thinking of a preacher you might like to consider. Of course, he isn't much to look at and seems to have eye trouble."

"I'm afraid that would rule him out from the start," Deacon A surmised.

"And he isn't much of a speaker, not an orator at all. Says you can't honor God with 'wisdom of words.' "

"But a preacher makes his living speaking, and people like a man who can give it out. Dr. Soundingbrass packs them in over at Memorial Church with his lectures on current events, and we don't want some fellow fumbling for words."

"The man I have in mind doesn't play up much to the pillars up at headquarters. In fact, he had a run-in with one of the main church leaders. Says he went off to a desert and got his doctrine all straightened out after he was called to preach."

"I don't know whom you are talking about," Deacon B put in, "but if a preacher is going to get anywhere he's got to stand in with the right authorities. That's what our head men are for, to see that the churches get the right preachers. Your preacher will never get promoted, rambling around out in a desert. This is an age of efficiency and you've got to use some business principles like we do in our workaday world."

"Oh, my man respects the fellows up at headquarters, but he says the same God who called them called him, and he gets his first orders direct from up higher."

"Mighty high-sounding to me," Deacon C grunted. "Where does he live?"

"He has no home, just travels about. He really stirs things up. They call him an upsetter."

"We don't need any more upsetting and disturbing preachers. Everything is upset now. We need a preacher who can keep harmony and not be stirring up the community. Might do for an evangelist, but even that is out of date these days. No, no, we don't want any sensationalists."

"He's an old-fashioned preacher, condemns false teaching. He wouldn't play ball with the liberalists, I'll tell you that. Believes in church discipline."

"Where have you been for the past fifty years? You sound like the horse-and-buggy age. That's all out. The new preaching has come to stay, and you might as well get in step with it. And we don't want any more church discipline. We had some of that here twenty-five years ago and never have got over it."

"I forgot to say my preacher has been in jail."

"What!" chimed all the Committee, "What do you mean, wasting our time? Are you trying to make a joke out of us?"

"Oh, no," the brother replied as he walked away. "You couldn't get this preacher, anyway. I was thinking of the Apostle Paul."

THE CORNER MAILBOX

IT WAS JUST an ordinary, unattractive corner mailbox, not much to look at. If it had been anything else I wouldn't have noticed it, but, being what it was, it was the object of my search. I wasn't looking for it because it was beautiful or because it was one of the scenic attractions. It did not appear deserving of much consideration, but when I reached it I entrusted to its care a very precious thing, a letter to my beloved.

Now, I wouldn't have deposited such a valuable missive just anywhere. I wouldn't have handed it over to a policeman or left it with the newsboy. I wouldn't even have given it to the bank. A bank is a much more impressive thing than a mailbox and we do commit some very important things to their keeping, but here I was passing all these places looking for a plain little old mailbox.

The mailbox is important, not because of what it is in itself, but because it belongs to, and is part of, something greater than itself. It is a unit in the great Postal System and I knew that, although that little mailbox, unassisted, could never deliver my letter to my beloved, it was part of a great movement that could.

Which set me thinking as I strolled on down the street. You and I are not much in ourselves, but when we get into the will of God and become part of His great purpose we assume an importance and share a responsibility infinitely beyond ourselves. This poor little mailbox could not get letters across the country and around the world, but it was part of something that could. When we yield to God and become co-workers and units in His great program, we become bearers of precious messages, channels of heavenly blessings, recipients of eternal grace, stewards of treasure in earthen vessels. Foolish things, weak and base, things that are not, all this we are in ourselves, but once we enter into the plan and purpose of God we assume a priceless value because of Him whose we are and Whom we serve.

This mailbox, set out in a field somewhere, disconnected from its system would be useless. It would neither receive nor transmit that stream of human communication for which it is made. Just so, many a life out of God's will, isolated and alone, living for self and none beside, just as if Jesus had never lived, just as if He'd never died—such a life can never be blessed nor be a blessing.

But look at the mailbox again. Suppose it complained and grumbled "Why did they ever set me on this dirty corner? I wanted so much to be up on the boulevard, among the bright lights and the fine shops, and here I am stuck in this dark, drab spot." But if it is in line with the postal system it can fulfill its function just the same, and the location doesn't make an awful lot of difference.

Do these lines fall under the eye of one who is restless, murmuring, inwardly wondering why God ever set you on such a corner? Are you tied down to drudgery, working among uncongenial companions, trying to preach in an unappreciative parish, or, maybe, an invalid sentenced to pass your days between bed sheets? Do not complain. There must be mailboxes on some dark corners, and when the final count is made perhaps the Great Postmaster will reward some obscure out-station for meritorious service beyond the intake and output up on the avenue. Stop being fretful and start being faithful over even a few things and you will be in line for heaven's promotion.

FACES IN THE FIRE

I AM BACK at the old home in the hills. It is springtime and beside me on the table is a little bouquet of bridal wreath and peach blossoms with their faint, intriguing fragrance that gently speaks of things sweet and pure and lovely in a world of blood and tears. What a blessed relief to turn from hearing news from the heart-rending avalanche of fire and sword to catch a whiff of April perfume and remember that after all the dictators have passed away the tender and the true will go on forever!

I have had my stroll this morning down around the creek and home again. The early haze of green along the watercourses is there once more. The grass has woven its magic carpet as of old. The yellow-hammer is making his spring announcements, the mockingbird has not forgotten his medley, the bluebird warbles just as others used to do. Cars and clothes, ladies' hats, and legislation may change but you can always depend on springtime in Carolina!

Last night I meditated awhile all alone in my little room in the old armchair that is battered by the years but still cozy. It was cool enough for a fire and there were glowing embers in the old fireplace and dancing shadows on the wall. A quiet evening among old memories is ever a boon to a weary traveler, and as one ponders the trail of the years back at the source where it started, there are always faces in the fire.

There's a wrinkled old face that looks back across the years as father comes to mind. There is an old letter here, written to me when I was a college freshman. "I'm expecting great things of you by and by," he tells me. I hope I have not disappointed him too much. There were times when he wondered, with abundant reason, just where my confused course might end. Eternity has erased the lines from his face, I am sure, and time has put some in my own, but of this I am confident, that the grace which brought him through danger, toil and snare will likewise bring me home.

There is another dear old face, not so long since removed, of an old-fashioned mother. How she would have been delighted in this visit of mine! She would be sitting right now in the chair over there, crutch in hand, basking in the account of my preaching travels. For however ordinary a preacher may be, a mother can magnify him to fill all her proportions and he who would never get a look from celebrity-chasers is a Spurgeon in the eyes of her who bore him. Mother never had much to say but she could say nothing more eloquently than some can lecture by the hour. Her calm appraisal of many a situation has relieved more than one fever of body and mind. What would we mortals do were it not for those whom God has enabled to recapture our true perspective for us once in a while?

Which brings to me another face in the fire, lovelier than all others of earth to me, tender with love and sweet solicitude. Says Alexander Whyte, "For in how many sloughs (of despond) do many men lie till this daughter of Help give them her hand, and out of how many more sloughs are they all their days by her delivered and kept!" Thank God for the women of His providence! And I am happy that this face in the fire is not a memory, for I am going to see Sara tomorrow!

There is a Face in the fire, loveliest of all. It is a face that was disfigured that I might be delivered, scarred that

I might be set free. God keep my heart and life that ever there shall be

> Nothing between my soul and the Saviour,
> So that His blessed face may be seen!

A WORD TO PROSPECTIVE MANIACS

I AM CONVINCED that if the devil cannot make us lazy, he will make us so busy here and there that the best is sacrificed for the good. I once thought that every invitation I received as a speaker was the leading of the Lord. But I discovered that I was sometimes invited to speak at two different places at the same time, and I knew that the Lord knew I was singular, not plural. From that, I went on to learn that I had been given some common sense and was expected to use it under the Spirit's direction.

We display the Lord's leading as much by what we refuse as by what we accept. The Lord is not interested in mere quantity production. We can often do more by doing less. It is no mark of godliness to be forever running about in a fever, our tongues hanging out, in a glorified St. Vitus's dance. These dear souls who argue that the devil never takes a vacation should remember that we are not supposed to imitate the devil. We follow the Lord, who was unhurried and who said, "Come ye yourselves apart and rest awhile."

It is high time we learned that in this nerve-wrecking, maddening modern rush, we have let the spirit of the times rob us utterly of meditation, devotion, rest, the passive side of our Christian experience without which we cannot be truly active to the glory of God. There is no depth to us. We are all whizzing around from preacher to preacher, meeting to meeting, with pad and pencil, hiding the Word in our notebooks instead of in our hearts. A lot of our Christian life and work is frothy, superficial, thin. We are growing mushrooms, not oaks.

I have learned long since that when I arrive in a place and calls descend like locusts to come to this meeting, grab a sandwich and hop to another, address the Whoozits at ten and the Whatsits at eleven, only to arrive at the main meeting woozy and exhausted, that part of a preacher's best equipment is a good healthy No. It looks good but it is a subtle snare, and both we and the good people who invite us are unwittingly deceived by it. If either we or they took second thought we could see that we defeat our own purposes when we spread ourselves too thinly, striking everywhere and hitting hard nowhere. We Christians often lead dissipated lives, squandering our energies in a multitude of good things but becoming so exhausted that none of it counts for much.

The temptation is great for an aggressive preacher to run a church, hold outside meetings, carry a radio program, put on a Bible school, edit a magazine, write books, and from there on add a new sideline every little while, until he ends up in a hospital. Once in a while there is a Hercules who can stand it, but is it the best way? The old saints did a few things well, as a rule. They took time to be still, and we go back to them now to feed our souls. They produced cream and it takes time for cream to rise.

If our lives and ministry count for anything today, we must solemnly resolve to make time for God. It is not easy. Some people won't like it, but somebody else wouldn't like it if we did some other way, so that doesn't matter. We must make out a schedule and work out a program at all costs that will eliminate the nonessential (including a lot of things some dear souls will think are very essential, put first things first, and make a lot of second-rate things stay in line, no matter how much they clamor for first place.

It is the best way to get to heaven without detouring by an insane asylum. And you will make a life as well as a living, and stay not only clothed but in your right mind.

FORGET NOT ALL HIS BENEFITS

LOOKING BACK across the years, I would say with the Psalmist, "Come and hear, all ye that fear God, and I will declare what he hath done for my soul." I cannot count my blessings nor name them one by one, but I am constantly being surprised at what the Lord has done. I have already enjoyed far more than I expected a few years ago. I can truly say that God has given me the desires of my heart.

I thank God for America. I would not want to be a man "with soul so dead who never to himself hath said, 'This is my own, my native land.'" We are infected today with a brand of pests who pretend to like it better the way they do it elsewhere. Some of us would gladly see them take a boat tomorrow for the land of their dreams if they don't like it here.

I am thankful for "Dixie-land, where I was born early on a frosty mornin'." I lived for five years in the heart of the Old South in Charleston, South Carolina. I know the jokes they tell on us Southerners, how we still fight the War Between the States. I trust I may not be accused of sectionalism, but I still like it best 'way down South.

I thank God that I grew up in the country, "far from the madding crowd's ignoble strife." God made the country and man made the town—and you certainly can see the difference! A country boy may learn city ways but a city boy cannot learn country ways—you have to be born and grow up in the country to be natural. Someone has said that city people and country folks are just ignorant on different subjects. I am grateful for memories of cotton fields and watermelon patches, for the oak trees in the front yard and the honeysuckle vine on the back porch, for the mockingbird in the morning, the wood thrush at sundown, and the whip-poor-will in the lone dark hills at night. I can still hear the night-hawk zooming in the evening summer sky, the crickets across the road, and the hoot owl in the deep woods giving me the shivers as I sat on the back porch pretending to wash my stub-toed feet before I went to bed. I thank God for the snowy world of winter and the miracle of spring, the good old summer time, and the tender wistfulness of autumn, "when the frost is on the 'punkin' and the fodder's in the shock." Often I have thought that if this world, marred and spoiled by sin, can be so lovely, what will the new earth be like when God has freed it from dictators, disease, death, and the devil and filled it with His glory as the waters cover the sea.

I am thankful for having had a Christian home. My parents took life seriously. Life was real and earnest, and the grave was not the goal. Father believed we came from somewhere and were going somewhere. There were foes to face and a flood to stem, and this poor world was no friend of grace to help us on to God. Like Noah, father got his family into the ark. I used to think he was a bit too strict, but I can see the point now. He could have compromised a little here and hedged a little there and dropped to the level of the average. He could have decided that maybe he was overdoing it and hidden behind the verse, "Be not righteous overmuch." But he was out to build with gold, silver, and precious stones and would not be inveigled into trafficking with wood, hay, and stubble. His life will stand the fire test, for he built soundly and managed to get some solid materials into the lives of his children as well.

I thank God for an experience of grace, which I have related elsewhere, and along with it a call to preach. I have enjoyed preaching. It may be misery to some, but I have not found it so. There are indeed ambassadors in bonds which they themselves have forged. Of course, if you are going to preach with one eye on a contrary deacon, if you are going to spend your time tickling the ears of a generation that cannot endure sound doctrine, if you are going to get your sermons from minister's manuals instead of digging into God's own storehouse as God's householder should do, if you are going to be that kind of preacher, you will never have liberty. No man can preach if he confers with flesh and blood for his authority. Let him go to Arabia and get his credentials from heaven. Let him shun Saul's armour and go after Goliath in his own native fashion and in the Name of the Lord. Blessed is God's ambassador who is not in bonds—bonds of habit, shackling sins of flesh or spirit, bonds within or bonds without, in his own family or church or among the ecclesiastics over him, bonds that quench the Spirit and stifle his message until he is a parrot instead of a prophet. Better live in the woods, eat berries, and drink spring water and keep one's own soul. We are in appalling need today of men who speak for God. Satan will try to scare any man who aspires to such a holy office. He hates a Micaiah who speaks only "what the Lord saith." He would make Baruchs of us all, feathering our nest in a world on fire. This is no time to hang up our stockings for the Santa Claus of this age to fill. Gehazi is all too prone to chase Naaman for a rake-off and bring upon himself the leprosy of God's judgment.

I thank God for friends, a host of them, whose prayers and provision have backed me up through the years. Their homes all over the land have opened to me. They have encouraged me and sometimes they have reproved, and I trust I have received both with appropriate grace. They listen to my sermons and read my books and bid me

Godspeed. Many of them I have never seen, but we are
bound together by the tie invisible. Eventually, many of
us will meet for the first time, and in Christ we are always
sure that Christians never meet for the last time!

But, above all, "thanks be unto God for his unspeakable
gift." Charles Kingsley, when he was asked what was the
secret of his beautiful life, answered, "I had a friend."
If my life ever approaches the beautiful it will be because

> I've found a Friend, O such a Friend!
> He loved me ere I knew Him;
> He drew me with the cords of love,
> And thus He bound me to Him.

Two boats passed each other on the Mississippi one
day, when an old colored workman on one pointed to
the other boat and said to a white passenger beside him,
"Look, there's the captain! Years ago, we were going along
like this when I fell overboard and the captain rescued
me. And ever since then I just loves to point him out!"

Once I was in waters too deep for my wit and will
to navigate, but the Captain of my salvation leaped overboard and came from heaven to earth to rescue me.

And since then I just love to point Him out.

JUST A CLOSER WALK WITH THEE

IT HAD BEEN a good week of preaching and teaching, a mountain-top experience in more ways than one. Hearts had been blessed. Decisions had been made. We came to Sunday morning and breakfast devotions. The kitchen help always sat in on that half hour of Bible meditation, prayer, and testimony.

That morning someone asked that Lena, the Negro cook, sing for us. I can see her now. She stood there in a corner, her arms folded, and began:

> Just a closer walk with Thee;
> Grant it Jesus, if you please.
> Daily walking close with Thee,
> Let it be, dear Lord, let it be.*

Immediately I sensed that the Spirit was present. My eyes grew moist. I sneaked out my handkerchief and looked sheepishly around—and, lo, my handkerchief was not the only one in action. The missionary near by was in tears. All over the crowded diningroom the fountains of the deep were broken up.

I noticed another thing. The Presbyterians were wiping their eyes just like the Baptists. The Methodists were as

* Negro Spiritual: Copyright by Harry W. Vom Bruch. Used by permission.

44

touched as the Brethren. I don't know how many denominations were represented that morning, but it made no difference now. Lena's song had lifted us above our fences and made us one. We might have argued about unification but here was unity. Lena's song did not create it, of course, but revealed it, for it is always there. The trouble is we are so dull and carnal that we forget it.

If we had spent that Sunday half hour in theological discussion, arguing prophecy or sanctification or church polity, we might have gone out upset and belligerent. I do not mean that these things are not important but more important still is "a closer walk with Thee."

Lena sang on:

> I am weak but Thou art strong.
> Jesus keeps me from all wrong.
> I'll be satisfied as long,
> As I walk, let me walk, close to Thee.

I said to myself: "This is it. Here we sit, Regulars and Irregulars, Independents and 'Dependents,' Stay-Inners and Come-Outers." Maybe if we could all get melted down in a closer walk with God we'd find that we aren't as far apart as we think. This fine old Negro had struck the Common Denominator. We could all get together on that song. She had done in a few minutes what a week of preaching and teaching hadn't done. Maybe she ought to go around to a lot of our hot and bothered gatherings and sound the keynote as she did on the mountain top that day. How often we fuss over what we think are "important issues" and then some simple soul puts us to shame and makes scholars take a back seat. Lena sang from her heart to our hearts, and we could stand a lot more of that. Too much of our worship today is from the head to the head.

Through this world of toil and snares,
If I falter, Lord, who cares,
Who with me my burden shares?
None but Thee, dear Lord, none but Thee.

We are lonely souls in a tortured world. And, dear Lord, our hearts are hungry for

Just a closer walk with Thee.

"HOW DID YOU GET ALONG?"

I AM HOMEWARD bound once more and riding on the old Carolina Special on a summer afternoon. I have just passed the little town of Newton, not far from my boyhood home. There is a new railroad station, built since my early days, but the old one still stands down the track a short distance away. As I rode by, I thought of days long past when I returned from preaching trips and father met me there.

I can see him yet standing by that old Ford in that unpressed blue serge suit. When I came up to where he stood he never failed to ask, "How did you get along?" It has been about twenty-five years since he last met me there. Time has done things to me, but of one thing I am glad—I am still doing what he always hoped I would do to the end. He should have been a preacher himself —two of his brothers were—and in me he sort of lived the life he knew he should have known himself. There was a time when the fire burned none too brightly, and great was his concern for fear that I should cease from doing what he had never begun to do.

But his prayers were not in vain and if he were living here now, nothing would make him happier than a recital of my preaching experiences. Just how it is where he now dwells I know only in part. How much he knows of what goes on here I cannot say. I do have a feeling that one day when I report to Headquarters he will be on hand

and it would seem just right to hear him say, "Well, how did you get along?"

He has had a lot to do with how I get along. He gave me a good start. He could think of nothing better for me than to preach the Gospel. And in that he was right. I tell young men never to aspire to be President if they can be preachers! Father believed that God still called His Samuels and felt that by Divine appointment preaching was first of all. He understood that it was time to confer with flesh and blood—if ever—after one had first conferred with God.

Whoever has not known the holy burden of a boy's future, whether his own boy's or someone else's, has missed much. To see a life unfold and witness the tug of war between God and Satan over the soul of a lad—there is no greater drama than that. And to help some youngster know God and live for Him—is there any nobler adventure?

As today, twenty-five years after, I ride past the old depot where so often Dad asked his question, my soul breathes a prayer that I may finish my course with joy. For what matters most in this brief pilgrimage is that we quit ourselves like men, that we do not disappoint those who dreamed largely and prayed hopefully for us when we gave scantiest promise—and, above all, that we be able to report well to the Great Overseer and merit His, "Well done." Blunders we shall make and failures will shame our faces and dampen our eyes. But if we can manage not to remember what we ought to forget and not to forget what we ought to remember, then forgetting the things behind and stirring up our minds by way of remembrance, we shall press on for the prize. It will pay off beyond all reckoning when we clasp hands with those loved long since and lost awhile and tell them how, by grace, we "got along."

A LETTER TO DAD

DEAR DAD:

Among the treasures of bygone years there's a faded old letter you wrote to me when I was a puzzled country boy away at college. I answered it then, but tonight, across the span of years, I'd like to answer it again. A lot of water has run under the bridge since, with scratchy pen, you put down those words of counsel to help me on the straight and narrow way. You have long since gone and I know you need no letter, for you see quite clearly from heaven's grandstand what is ofttimes so foggy to us who still run the race. A letter from me can give you little information, but one from you could certainly throw light on many a subject!

But just the same, I'd like to thank you better than ever I did when you were here for what you did and what you were. I am so glad that you believed the authority in the home belonged to you and not to me. I remember that time when your little boy tried just once to talk out loud to another little boy at church and disturbed the service. You handled that well: I never talked out again! I thank you for reading the Bible at bedtime before the old fireplace and then on bended knee committing us all afresh to our Father in heaven. My knees grew tired sometimes, but you built a wall around my soul that the devil was never able to tear down. I know you never kept up with the styles, and that funny fur cap I wore off to boarding school lingers still in my recollections: but I never knew the difference then and I get a good laugh out of it now, so no harm was done. You didn't have a lot to sell in your grocery store, but you gave away a lot in helpful words and godly counsel: you cast your bread upon the waters and some of it is coming back still today.

I remember the times I overheard you praying in that little store, reminding God that you had given me to Him and asking Him to remember His Word to you in which He had caused you to hope. I think you got a little shaky about me a time or two: it looked as if I were going to miss the track in spite of everything, but God didn't let you down, for He never lets anyone down. I'm preaching that old-time religion that you always hoped I'd always preach and partly because my father's prayers have followed me. As I look back over the road I've come and see how near I came to leaving it, I know that something greater than myself had a hand in it all; yes, not something but Some One, for the God of my father had an understanding with you and His eye was on me.

I've thought a lot of how you used to meet me when I came home from my preaching trips. When the train rounded that curve at the depot I could always see you standing beside the little old Ford, in that old blue suit that never was pressed again from the day you bought it. It never seems right to round that curve and not see you there. But there are other curves ahead, and when I get home for good I don't know how close to the gate of glory you can stand, but I'm sure you'll be on hand. I have wondered what you'll look like, but I'm sure I'll know you. And there'll be plenty of time to catch up on the conversation that was interrupted years ago.

You always liked to sing, though neither of us was unusually gifted that way. I am sure you're in great trim now, after all these years of practice. I am anxious to get over there and try out my brand-new voice with you on "Amazing Grace, How Sweet the Sound." From the looks of things down here, it probably won't be long till Jesus comes. I'll see you in the morning!

ARE YOU "THERE"?

And the word of the Lord came unto him (Elijah),
saying, Get thee hence and turn thee eastward, and hide
thyself by the brook Cherith, that is before Jordan. And
it shall be, that thou shalt drink of the brook; and I have
commanded the ravens to feed thee THERE. . . .

Arise, get thee to Zarephath, which belongeth to Zidon,
and dwell THERE: behold, I have commanded a widow
woman THERE to sustain thee. So he arose and went
to Zarephath. And when he came to the gate of the city,
behold, the widow woman was THERE . . ."

(I KINGS 17: 2-4, 9, 10).

I DO NOT believe that the ravens would have fed Elijah
anywhere else, nor would the widow woman have appeared
anywhere else except *"there."* God did not say, "Elijah,
ramble around as you please and I will provide for you."
"There" was the place of God's will for Elijah—the place
of His Purpose, the place of His Power and the place
of His Provision.

"There" was the place of God's purpose. God has a
"there" for you, somewhere He wants you to be, something
He wants you to do. You can never be truly happy elsewhere, nor can you please God anywhere but "there."
You may do lovely things and become a "success," but
always there will be the haunting sense of having chosen
life's second best.

Sir Thomas Lipton, the English sportsman, won many yachting prizes, but he never could capture the American cup. One day, showing a friend his glittering collection of trophies, he suddenly said, with a wave of the hand, "And I'd give them all for the one I didn't get!" So, however many of earth's awards and crowns we may gain, if we miss the reward of God's approval, the prize of the high calling of God in Christ Jesus, we shall feel at the close of our day that we would gladly give them all for the one we missed. Woodrow Wilson spoke of "being defeated by one's secondary successes." Verily, we are cheated when we choose our own way, whatever we may attain in it, if we miss the purpose of God.

"There" is the place of blessing. When Jacob wandered from Bethel and trouble descended upon him at Shalem, God commanded him, *"Arise, go up to Bethel and dwell there"* (GENESIS 35:1). Sometimes we go back to Bethel during the revival but we do not dwell there.

"There" is not a particular emotional experience; it is simply the place of God's will. David *"served his generation by the will of God"* (ACTS 13:36), and in so doing he proved that he was "there." Epaphras prayed that the saints might *"stand perfect and complete in all the will of God"* (COLOSSIANS 4:12), in other words, that they might be "there." Our Lord could say to the Father, *"I have glorified thee on the earth; I have finished the work which thou gavest me to do"* (JOHN 17:4). He was always "there"!

God has a Cherith and a Zarephath for you. It may be across the street, it may be across the sea. Some sing, "I'll go where you want me to go, dear Lord," but they are not willing to stay where He wants them to stay. A radio preacher tells of receiving a letter from a young lady who was sure that she could do great things for the Lord if she could move to Pittsburgh, but was sure she could do nothing in the small town where she was. It developed that she refused to work in the small tasks in her home church because she felt too big for it. We have plenty of "Pittsburgh Christians," eagles on hummingbird nests, always too big for where they are.

In the account of the Great Commission, we overlook the setting: *"Then the eleven disciples went away into Galilee, into a mountain where Jesus had appointed them"* (MATTHEW 28:16). They were in the place of the Divine appointing, therefore they received the Divine appointment. Some of us have had no commission because we are not "there," at the place of His appointing.

In the second place, "there" was the place of God's power. I do not believe that the miracle of the ravens and the meal barrel would have occurred anywhere but "there." Men wonder why they never feel God's power or see any evidences of His working. It is because they are out of His purpose, not in His will. We say, "What power Elijah had!" but he had no power in himself, he was simply "there," in the place of power. We might say, "What power that radio has!" "What power that electric light has!" But they are very frail contraptions, they are simply in the place of power, connected with the source. When the traffic officer stops you as you drive down the street, it is not his strength that does it; you could drive over him. It is his authority that makes you halt; he represents something greater than himself. So we are nothing in ourselves, but when we are in the place of God's purpose we have His power, and greater is He that is in us than he that is in the world.

Men have wondered at the power of George Muller. He had no power of himself; he was simply "there," in the place of God's purpose for George Muller. Hudson Taylor said he once thought God was looking for men strong enough to use, but he learned that God was looking for men weak enough to use. The lad who supplied the loaves and fishes for the feeding of the multitude would have been nonplussed if you had told him that morning that he had enough food for several thousand people. He did not know what he had until Jesus took it and broke it and blessed it and passed it around. Nor do you know what you have until you give it to the Lord.

Only when we are "there," in the place of His purpose, are we in the place of His power. Samson did a great many remarkable things, but he never was much; he did not stay "there." He may have looked better after his haircut but he lost his strength. Too many Christians let the world give them a haircut. One day they carry off the gates of Gaza, but next day they may be in the lap of Delilah; they do not abide in Christ, they do not stay "there."

There is no place "just as good" as "there," the place of God's purpose. We try to strike bargains with the Lord, offer to do something else, seek a compromise or substitute. We work terribly hard at something that may be fine and lovely, but it is not His choice and inwardly we are rebellious. A minister brother tells of a stubborn youngster in a home who was told by his mother to sit down. He refused twice, and then she made him sit down; but he said, "Mother, I may be sitting down but I'm standing up inside!" So often do we seem to be yielded to God and living "there," but there is inward rebellion. And God rates rebellion as a grievous thing: *"For rebellion is as the sin of witchcraft and stubbornness is as iniquity and idolatry"* (I SAMUEL 15:23).

Finally, "there" was the place of God's provision. There would have been no bread, no flesh, no meal, for Elijah anywhere but "there." "Where God guides, He provides" is a well-worn proverb but gloriously true. Notice that God said, "I have commanded the ravens to feed thee there"; "I have commanded a widow woman there to sustain thee." Elijah had gone on ahead and made arrangements. Strange arrangements they were—I doubt that stranger arrangements ever were made for boarding a preacher! But the plan worked, as it always does when God is in it. He is responsible for our upkeep when we follow

His directions, but He is not responsible for any expenses not included in His schedule.

Elijah began his interview with the widow by asking, like our Lord at the well of Samaria, for a drink of water. You will observe that when Elijah found this woman, she was engaged at a menial task, gathering sticks, but before he left she had seen the miraculous. From the menial to the miraculous! So our Lord found Peter fishing for fish and made him a fisher of men; found Matthew collecting taxes and made him a Gospel writer. If we are faithful in the least, God will show us much. Fetching a drink of water does not cost much, although a cup of water given in His Name shall not be unrewarded. But it does not test faith, so Elijah asked next for a morsel of bread and the first cake at that. Now it looked as though there would be only one cake, so here was a real test for the widow woman. Alas, we give God the crumbs, not the cake; the scraps and fragments and leftovers of time and thought and talent and money. Malachi reproved the Jews in his day who kept the good animals given them for sacrifice and gave the Lord the sick and crippled. How he might thunder at us today who give God the crumbs from our tables and eat the cake ourselves!

The widow woman was fearful, but Elijah reassured her: "Fear not . . . for thus saith the Lord . . ." God had promised to provide and that was enough.

> In some way or other, the Lord will provide.
> It may not be my way, it may not be thy way.
> And yet in His own way, the Lord will provide.

Of course, God did not fill the barrel, as we Americans would demand; He simply supplied enough. He has promised to supply our needs, not our wants (PHILIPPIANS 4:19). So long as we are in His will, we shall have health enough, time enough, work enough, money enough to do what He wants done. Why should we want any more?

And He never asks us to do more than we can do by His grace. He may seem to ask the impossible and we may be sure that we are going to fail, but if we are willing to fail for God, we won't fail. Nobody ever failed who was honest with God.

How we do let circumstances blind us to the all-sufficiency of God! I think of the morning when Elisha's servant must have walked out on the back porch and discovered an army sent to capture the great prophet. (In those days God's preachers were such troublemakers that they sent the militia after them.) The servant was horrified to see soldiers to the right of him, soldiers to the left of him, soldiers before him, soldiers everywhere. But Elisha came out calmly, and instead of bothering to look around him, he looked higher and saw angels to the right of him, angels to the left of him, angels before him, angels everywhere, for the angels of the Lord were encamping round about him who feared God to deliver him. No wonder Elisha could pray for this frightened servant's eyes to be opened that he might see! And we need such an eye opener today.

Yes, when we are "there," in the place of God's purpose, we are in the place of His power and provision. Are you "there"? A little girl in a Midwestern city came forward one night after I had preached from this text and whispered in my ear, "I'm here but I'm afraid I'm not there." Many of us are "here," among those present, but we are not "there," in the place of His choosing. We may be "there" the moment we resign the right to our own lives and let Him take control. Do not grow uneasy if guidance does not come in a moment. What He wants is your yielded will, and the minute you give Him that, you are "there," although it may be some time before He shows you just where it is geographically.

May I relate to you a chapter out of my own experience? I began to preach when I was a boy. After four years of preaching, I went away to school and in the period that followed I became unsettled in my beliefs. I felt, under modernistic and liberal influences, that I should adapt the Gospel to the modern mind, which, by the way, is not very modern and not much mind. There came a day when my ministry failed and I returned to my old country home in the hills. That winter my father died and I was left with my mother, having only a country grocery store as our support, and that was robbed and burned to the ground in the following spring! During those months the Lord spoke to my soul and led me to see that if I returned to the old Gospel and preached it, He would clear the track for me. So I renounced the "new approach" and got into the Cherith and Zarephath of God's will for me. First, I had to return to the church where I had preached the "new position" and give them the message God had given me. The way has not always been easy, but I can testify that God had gone before and made arrangements. I have found "there" to be the place of His abundant power and marvelous provision. The years since that experience have been one continued story of "meal in a barrel."

Are you "there"?

FOOLS, FACTS AND FIRE

Fools for Christ's sake. (I CORINTHIANS 4:10).
Preach the Word. (II TIMOTHY 4:2).
Stir up the gift of God. (II TIMOTHY 1:6).

OVER THIRTY YEARS ago, in the foothills of the Blue Ridge Mountains, alone in the woods on a summer afternoon, I came to Christ and believed His promise, "Him that cometh unto me I will in no wise cast out." I had been brought up in a Christian home, under old-fashioned preaching—sin black, hell hot, judgment certain, eternity long, and salvation free. I was converted during an old-fashioned revival—not a modern, fashionable, harmless little revival, but an old-fashioned revival that stirred the saints and saved sinners and set the angels rejoicing and put the devil's program in reverse. I mean an old-fashioned "Amazing Grace," "How Firm a Foundation," "Blest Be the Tie That Binds" sort of revival, where "grace taught our hearts to fear and grace our fears relieved; how precious did that grace appear the hour we first believed!" They didn't "hold" revivals in those days, they turned them loose!

I do not remember that any particular sermon brought me under conviction. I knew that I was lost, that Christ died for me, and that the gift of God was eternal life. My father and mother taught me that and prepared me for that summer afternoon when I simply took God at His Word and, after all,

> What more can He say than to us He hath said,
> To us who for refuge to Jesus have fled?

I remember that I came back home through the woods to my father's little shop, and I didn't go in through the door—I went through the window and we embraced each other in the joy of my new experience. That was back in the days before the devil had a monopoly on enthusiasm. That was before these strange times came along, when sinners can weep in theaters over the glycerin tears of Hollywood divorcées, while the saints are ashamed to weep in church over a lost and dying world.

That afternoon I went out at supper time to do the chores, and I went singing:

> Jesus, I my cross have taken,
> All to leave and follow Thee;
> Destitute, despised, forsaken,
> Thou from hence my all shalt be.

If I didn't have much theology in my head, I had a lot of doxology in my heart! I have often thought since that I could take half a dozen of those old-fashioned, red-hot Christians of those days, who knew but two or three things but knew them through and through and up and down and in and out—that I could take a few of those old Christians and go places for God while a lot of modern church members are discussing ways and means, pouring hot chocolate, and reading the minutes of the last meeting!

Since my conversion, I have had the usual ups and downs of a Christian and a preacher trying to get located in the jig-saw puzzle of the present-day confusion of the saints. I have mixed and mingled with all shades and grades and varieties and degrees, from the Big Shots—some of whom turn out to be just buckshot when you get to know them!—down to some who have never learned that it takes more than a three-cornered hat to make a Napoleon out of a corporal! I have worked in different kinds of churches. I have labored with those Sunday-morning saints whose religion consists of a little Ladies' Aid, lemonade, and a little money in a duplex envelope. For a while I was among the modernists. At one time I thought I didn't know enough to be a modernist, but eventually I discovered that you don't have to know much!

Finally, by the grace of God, I landed among the fundamentalists. "Landed" may not be the right word, for a lot of them are still at sea! I have never been able to understand why they call us fundamentalists a dull and colorless crowd. I think we are the most interesting collection of human specimens that ever came along. There are, for instance, the professional come-outers, religious gypsies, church grasshoppers who never can find a church or preacher good enough for them. They remind us of the old brother who used to sing above everybody else and completely out of tune:

> Sweet prospects, sweet birds and sweet flowers
> Have all lost their fragrance BUT ME!

It was one of this sort who had already belonged to three denominations and was getting ready to join a fourth. He announced his intention to his pastor *pro tem,* for any pastor he had was *pro tem!* The old pastor, wise to the ways of all such, replied, "Well, I don't think it does any harm to change labels on an empty bottle!"

Then we have the porcupine Christians—they have a lot of good points but you can't get near them!

And by the time you have listened to one crowd explain the two natures and another the three natures; one crowd explain why the church will go through the great tribulation and another explain why it will not; one crowd explain why the Roman Empire will be revived and another explain why it will not; one crowd explain why we may have a revival and another why we will not—by the time you have listened to all that, you will readily agree that while we may lack a lot of things in the camp of the fundamentalists, variety is not one of them!

But "with all their faults, I love them still" (of course, most of them are not very still), because I feel that most of them have the root of the matter in them. Sometimes they grow pretty stubborn, like the Scotsman who said he was open to conviction but would like to see the man who could convince him! And some of them do funny things, like getting out on a limb with Mussolini (I don't think Mussolini has caused the Italian nation half the embarrassment he has caused some Bible teachers!). But for a' that, I love them still, for they believe in the Book, the Blood and the Blessed Hope, and I expect to see them all get together in heaven, even if they can't do it down here.

But sometimes I do wish that these dividers of the Word, who take it apart much better than they ever get it back together, would agree a little better. Just when I am stretched out and resting on some good verse, some expositor shows up like a policeman to order me off private property and tell me that this verse is reserved for the Jew and that for the Kingdom Age. I have heard of a man without a country and I had almost decided once that these Word-Dividers were going to leave me a preacher without a Bible, and I began to wonder, "Is this the communion of saints or the confusion of tongues?" Finally, I took refuge in the text: "Let God be true, but every man a liar."

Sometimes I have thought that I'd like to go back again to the old days at Corinth Baptist Church, where I grew up, where we used to enjoy the spiritual food without arguing too much about the recipe. I have noticed that folks who are most finicky about their food usually have dyspepsia. Two things make a good meal, good food and a good appetite. And the best preparation for the Bread of Life is a good, hearty appetite.

Josh Billings is reported to have said, "I'd rather know a few things for certain than be sure of a lot of things that ain't so." There are a few things I believe for certain, and I leave you to quibble over the details. For one thing, I am certain that the Bible is the Word of God. Either it is or it isn't, and either all of it is the Word of God or we never can be sure of any of it. It is either absolute or obsolete. If we have to start changing this verse, toning down that, apologizing for this and making allowances for that, we might as well give up, so we must take it as it is or leave it alone.

I believe, furthermore, that "all have sinned," that man is lost and in need of a Saviour. I must confess that I am not much impressed with the human race. The heart is deceitful and desperately wicked and man is no better than he ever was. His head and hands have outrun his heart, and if you scratch off the varnish of civilization, you discover the same old savage, who has merely discovered more terrible ways of being low-down and horrible. For further information read your newspaper! I never say that civilization is going to the dogs. I still have some respect for dogs. Mankind without the grace of God is doing things beneath the dignity of the beasts of the field. I read a story of a hog that got drunk, and when the other hogs would have nothing to do with him, he said, "If you'll excuse me for acting like a man, I never will do it again!"

But I also believe that "God so loved the world that he gave his only begotten Son." I have read books and heard sermons on the atonement and most of them have confused more than they have clarified. It is always easier to understand what the Bible says than to understand what somebody thinks it meant to say. Barabbas should have had a clear understanding of the atonement, for he could

have said literally. "He put himself in my place," and
that is what Christ did for us all.

> Upon a life I did not live;
> Upon a death I did not die,
> Another's life, Another's death,
> I stake my whole eternity.

And then I am so glad that "whosoever believeth on
Him shall not perish but have everlasting life." I am so
glad that it is not "whosoever feeleth a certain way, whosoever seeth a vision or dreameth a dream or prayeth
through." What a time I used to have trying to understand
what the brethren meant by "saving faith"! I grew up
in the county next to A. C. Dixon's home county in North
Carolina, and have preached in churches his father used
to serve. I have thought often of how as a boy he read
Pilgrim's Progress and was brought into a miserable frame
of mind. He cried because he couldn't cry, was burdened
because he wasn't burdened, distressed because he wasn't
distressed. Finally, he went to church, and after his father
had preached on how to be saved, Clarence went to the
mourner's bench, and when his father came along and
asked how it was with him, he replied that he was trusting
Jesus and his father made it plain that that was all he
was expected to do. How many grow confused right there
and try to have faith in their faith instead of faith in
the Lord!

These are a "few things for certain" which I believe
with all my heart. There is much that I don't understand;
if I could understand it, there wouldn't be much in it!
I don't understand predestination but I believe that I am
chosen in Him. I don't understand all about the security
of the saints but I believe that I am a child of God and
that, while my Father may discipline me, He will never
disown me. I am not an expert in prophecy but I am
not looking for the kingdom without the King. I know

that some make a glorified hobby of prophecy, being occupied with His coming but not occupying till He come. I know that some are always studying the meaning of the fourth toe of the right foot of some beast in prophecy and have never used either foot to go and bring men to Christ. I do not know who the 666 is in Revelation but I know this world is sick, sick, sick, and the best way to speed the Lord's return is to win more souls for Him. I could lecture on "The Rise and Fall of Hitler's Mustache" and get a crowd, but if I spoke on "Obedience" you couldn't get some saints out to church with a rope and tackle. They don't believe in amusements but they want to be amused!

Now, if you ask me, "What is the supreme need of the hour?" I would say, in the light of our texts, that we need *fools* for Christ's sake with the *facts* of the Word set on *fire* from Above.

There is something lacking among Bible Christians today. If you are aware of it, I need not describe it; if you are not aware of it, you would not understand if I did describe it. I have no fancy name for it. You may call it "the filling of the Spirit," "full surrender," "consecration," "the victorious life," "revival." Unfortunately, too many of us have argued over the expressions without having the experience. Whatever it is, most of us haven't it! Let us put it this way, that we need a new experience of the Lord in the hearts of His people.

Too much of our orthodoxy is correct and sound but, like words without a tune, statutes without songs, it does not glow and burn, it does not stir the wells of the heart, it has lost its hallelujah, it is too much like a catechism and not enough like a camp meeting. You may smile at our spiritual forbears, call them primitive and antiquated; but they had a vividness and a vitality, a fervor and a fire, that make us look like fireflies beside their flaming torches. One man with a glowing experience of God is worth a library full of arguments.

We need a heart warming. It is one thing to commemorate Aldersgate and talk about what God did to John Wesley; it is another thing to have our own hearts strangely warmed. The early Christians did not need a shot in the arm every Sunday to keep them going. They knew Jesus and they upset the world and worried the devil and gave wicked rulers insomnia and started something that jails couldn't lock up, fire couldn't burn, water couldn't drown, swords couldn't kill. The church needs dare-saints instead of more diplomats. This world has never been moved by cold, calculating brass hats but by *fools,* with their *facts* on *fire.*

You may belittle experience and speak of the dangers of emotion, but we are suffering today from a species of Christianity as dry as dust, as cold as ice, as pale as a corpse, and as dead as King Tut. We are suffering, not from a lack of correct heads but of consumed hearts. Alexander Maclaren said:

"There is a type of intellectual preacher who is always preaching down enthusiasm and preaching up what they call sober standards of feeling in matters of religion, by which in nine cases out of ten they mean exactly such a tepid condition as is described in much less polite language when the voice of heaven says, 'Because thou art neither cold nor hot but lukewarm, I will spew thee out of my mouth.' It was not Erasmus, the polished, learned, scintillating, mighty intellect of his time, who made Germany over; it was rough, rugged Martin Luther with a conviction and compassion as deep as life."

God forgive us, in an hour like this, that we have been dry Christians, preaching a dynamite Gospel and living firecracker lives. Let us get alone with God, confess our sins, claim the cleansing blood, be filled with the Spirit, and go out to be Christ's *fools,* with our *facts* on *fire!*

GOD'S "INEVITABLE PROGRESS"

FOR SOME YEARS before the bottom fell out of civilization we heard much about the inevitability of progress. The evolutionists with all their kith and kin assured us that man was as sure to move forward as the sparks to fly upward. We have not heard much of that lately. The only inevitability now mentioned is that of world destruction, at least the possibility of the extermination of the human race.

With the wiseacres now looking for a hole in the ground in which to escape from their own inventions, it is very evident that if we are progressing it is in reverse. Instead of creating a millennium we have contrived a madhouse.

But there is one kind of progress that is sure. The eternal purpose of God moves on. God's program is running on schedule. He will arrive where He is going. Let us consider three ways in which the growth of God's purpose is revealed. *The God-Man grew on. God's men grow on. God's message grows on.*

First, *The God-Man grew on.* Almost two thousand years ago God solved the greatest problem of all time, how to be a just God and yet justify ungodly men. How can a holy God and unholy men be brought together? Something had to be done about the sin problem. There was nothing that man could do. But God so loved the world that He gave His only begotten Son. When we were without strength, in due time Christ died for the ungodly. There had to be someone who was both God and man to bring together God and men. God solved that problem by sending his Son, who had no sin in Him but took all sin on Him, was made sin for us though He knew no sin, that we might be made the righteousness of God in Him.

So He came, born of a woman, and was laid in a manger in Bethlehem. Of course, the devil was not asleep. He got busy immediately to try to destroy the God-Man. King Herod was his instrument. All the children two years old and under in that part of the country were slain. But Joseph and Mary, warned of God, fled with the baby Jesus to Egypt. There they stayed until Herod died and the angel advised Joseph to return, "for," said he, "they are dead which sought the young child's life." They always die who run against the purposes of God!

Then we read that the child Jesus was taken to Nazareth, and Luke tells us: *"And the child grew and waxed strong in spirit, filled with wisdom: and the grace of God was upon him; and Jesus increased in wisdom and stature, and in favor with God and man."* The God-Man grew on and grew up, died and rose again, and accomplished our redemption. God's purpose prevailed, the devil was defeated, Herod died. But *The God-Man grew on.* Little did proud Rome know, little did cultured Greece imagine, little did religious Israel suspect, little did poor Nazareth dream, that in that little village, working at a carpenter's bench, was the Son of God and Son of man. Even a worthy Israelite asked, "Can there any good thing come out of Nazareth?" Indeed, all that is good came out of Nazareth, for in Him dwelt all the fulness of the Godhead bodily.

In the second place, *God's men grow on.* In the Old Testament we read of the boy Samuel whose mother gave him to the Lord even before his birth. After he came she took him up to Eli the priest at Shiloh, and there he grew up. It was an evil age. Eli was old and his sons were immoral and the nation was backslidden. The calamity howlers and viewers-with-alarm, no doubt, were lamenting that the good old days were gone forever. But amidst all the sin and shame, the impurity and the infidelity, we read, *"And the child Samuel grew on, and was in favor both with the Lord, and also with men,"* reminding us of the similar verse about the child Jesus. God had His eye on that boy, for His eyes run to and fro throughout the whole earth, waiting to show Himself strong in behalf of those whose heart is perfect toward Him. Then came the night when God called and Samuel answered, and we read after that, *"And Samuel grew, and the Lord was with him, and did let none of his words fall to the ground."* Thus began a glorious career as the last of the judges, counselor of kings, and spokesman for God. *God's man Samuel grew on.*

In the New Testament there is a similar statement. It was another evil day. For years there had been no prophet in Israel, and the fire of the Spirit had died low. God's people lived under a heathen power and religion and had sunk into dead formalism. But God sent to earth another boy to grow up outdoors and be the forerunner of the God-Man Himself. We read of John the Baptist that *"The child grew, and waxed strong in spirit, and was in the deserts till the day of his shewing unto Israel."* God's man John the Baptist grew on!

So it has been through the centuries. There has never been a time so dark and dismal and desolate but somewhere God had a boy growing on. Remember that the days were dreary and the outlook desperate while the boy Martin Luther grew on. And the boy John Wesley, and the boy George Whitefield, and the boy George Fox, and the boy Charles Haddon Spurgeon, and the boy Dwight L. Moody. If you had seen any of these at the age when God called Samuel, you might not have suspected that here was God's man growing on. In Wales a lad in the coal mines prayed for years that God might endue him with the Spirit for revival. God heard him, for Evan Roberts was God's man growing on to spark the great Welsh awakening.

One thinks of the feeding of the five thousand. Here is an emergency, a multitude hungry and without food. But there are no unforeseen emergencies with God. Andrew reports, *"There is a lad here* which hath five barley loaves and two small fishes." Ah, God has a boy on the spot! Of course, Philip took a dark view of the possibilities: "But what are they among so many?" But when this boy gave to Jesus such as he had, and all he had, the miracle happened.

Preaching is such a thrilling business. When my eye runs over the congregation and I see boys scattered here and there, I take heart. There may be a Samuel growing up among them! There may be a John the Baptist down there getting ready to be a voice in the wilderness. Never mind if he is not brilliant or prepossessing. He may have but loaves and fishes, but "little is much if God is in it," and that light lunch blessed and broken and distributed by the Lord will feed a multitude. Never take your congregation lightly, though it be small and unimpressive; one of God's men may be growing up in it.

What a challenge to every parent who has a child in the home! He may be God's man growing on. Give him every needed counsel and correction, teach him to listen when God speaks. No man or woman ever had a nobler challenge or a higher privilege than to bring up a child for God, and whenever we slight that privilege or neglect that ministry for anything else, we live to mourn it in heartache and grief. There were many things that my father did not have, but one thing he did have: he had a consuming ambition that in his home a boy should grow up to live for God.

God's men grow on but God expects some assistance from us in helping them to grow on.

An old man going on a lone highway
Came in the evening cold and grey
To a chasm yawning both deep and wide.

The old man crossed in the twilight dim;
That swollen stream was naught to him.
But he stopped when safe on the other side
And built a bridge to span the tide.
"Old man," said a fellow traveler near,
"You are wasting your time in labor here;
Your journey will end with the closing day,
You never again will pass this way.
You've crossed the chasm deep and wide.
Why build you this bridge at eventide?"
The laborer lifted his old grey head:
"Good friend, in the way I have come," he said,
"There followeth after me today
A youth whose feet must pass this way.
This chasm which has been naught to me
To that fair youth may a pitfall be.
He too must cross in the twilight dim;
Good friend, I am building this bridge for him."

Yes, *God's men grow on,* and blessed is he who has a part in their progress.

Finally, I would have you observe that *God's message grows on.* We have already seen how one King Herod tried to destroy the child Jesus, but, instead, died himself while the *God-Man* grew on. Years later, another Herod tried to stop the progress of the early church by killing James and putting Peter in prison. A little later, we read that "the angel of the Lord smote him . . . and he was eaten of worms, and gave up the ghost," and then, in striking contrast, it is declared, *"But the word of God grew and multiplied."* Herods rise and fall, but God's message grows on. The kings of the earth set themselves and the rulers take counsel together against the Lord and against His anointed, but what happens? The worms get them, not only in body but also in soul, where the worm dieth not and the fire is not quenched. And under the epitaph of every enemy of the Gospel we may add, *"But the word of God grew and multiplied."*

When the power of God fell on Ephesus under the ministry of Paul, we read that fear fell on them all, and the name of the Lord Jesus was magnified; that many believed and confessed and burned their evil books, and again there follows the comment, *"So mightily grew the word of God and prevailed."* The very essence of a spiritual awakening is this, that *God's message grows on.*

Here is a progress that is really inevitable. "For as the rain cometh down, and the snow from heaven, and returneth not thither, but watereth the earth, and maketh it bring forth and bud, that it may give seed to the sower, and bread to the eater; *so shall my word be* that goeth forth out of my mouth: it shall not return unto me void; but it shall accomplish that which I please, and it shall prosper in the thing whereto I sent it." There may be setbacks and temporary defeats. God's message may seem to lose some battles but it will not lose the war!

Someone stood on an ocean beach and observed the incoming tide. Wave after wave broke on the sands, but the tide came in on schedule! Out of that experience grew a blessed illustration of how God's message always wins:

On the far reef the breakers recoil in shattered foam;
Yet still the sea behind them urges its forces home;
Its chant of triumph surges through all the thunderous din,
The wave may break in failure but the tide is sure to win.

O mighty sea, thy message in changing spray is cast:
Within God's plan of progress it matters not at last,
How wide the shores of evil, how strong the reefs of sin;
The wave may be defeated but the tide is sure to win.

Amid all the wreckage of civilization today one thing stands eternally certain: the purpose of God will prevail. We see not yet all things put under Him, but we see

Jesus. The God-Man, God's men, and God's message are bound to win. Some may object by saying that there are more heathen now than ever, that there is more sin than ever, that the world is farther from being converted than ever. That is just another proof of the truth of our proposition. God's Word never said the world would be converted but that perilous, not prosperous, times shall come in the last days, that evil men will wax worse and worse, that because lawlessness shall abound, the love of most will wax cold. And it declares that just as the God-Man Christ Jesus came on time when first He came in grace, so He will come on time when He comes again in glory.

I would warn you, however, on one point. Just because God's plan and purpose are sure to win does not mean that you are to sit idly by and watch it win. God works His plan by working His people. The God-Man finished His work as our Saviour, but the proclamation of that finished work is not finished. God's men grow on, but we can help them grow on in a thousand ways. God's message grows on, but it grows as we go to take it and to send it.

It is a dark hour and the only light today is provided by the God-Man, who said, "I am the light of the world"; by God's men, of whom He said, "Ye are the light of the world"; and by God's message, of which it is said, "The entrance of thy words giveth light." We are to *see the light* when we look unto Jesus in saving faith. We are to *be a light,* for He told us to let our light shine before men; and we are to *send the light* to the people in darkness, for how shall they hear without a preacher and how shall they preach except they be sent?

Here is the unbeatable combination, God's winning team; the God-Man, God's men, and God's message. Here is the only inevitable progress. Here is the one growing movement that will not die. Long ago the enemies of the Gospel were baffled even then because they could not stop it: prison doors would not stay shut, nor would the mouths of Gospel preachers. We read that the puzzled rulers *doubted . . . whereunto this would grow.* Well, it is still growing and if we do not grow with it we die. Make sure that you are born into it and that as it grows you grow in grace and in the knowledge of our Lord and Saviour Jesus Christ.

GAMALIEL, THE APPEASER

NOBODY EVER CALLED the Acts of the Apostles a dull book. Something is happening in it every minute. These early Christians, on fire for God, tackled the world, the flesh and the devil in a head-on collision and soon got into plenty of trouble.

By the time we reach the fifth chapter this trouble has assumed several forms. The chapter begins with trouble inside the church: "But a certain man named Ananias, with Sapphira his wife . . ." The church has always been harmed most by trouble within, but at this time it was not so anemic as now and the poison was soon cleared.

Then trouble looms again on the outside. Peter and the apostles are again brought before the council, the religious authorities. True Christianity through the ages has always clashed with organized religion. Peter and the apostles minced no words. Their speech is a classic: "We ought to obey God rather than men. The God of our fathers raised up Jesus, whom ye slew and hanged on a tree. Him hath God exalted with his right hand to be a Prince and a Saviour, for to give repentance to Israel, and forgiveness of sins. And we are his witness of these things; and so is also the Holy Ghost, whom God hath given to them that obey him."

No wonder the council was "cut to the heart"! A sermon like that, with the Trinity in it, Calvary in it, the resurrection in it, repentance in it, forgiveness in it, the gift of

75

the Spirit in it, plainly charging the rulers with murder and boldly claiming to be Christ's witnesses—and all in four verses!—a sermon like that was bound to cut to the heart even a religious council, often the hardest crowd on earth to move.

Trouble within, trouble without. And now comes another kind of trouble in disguise, trouble on the fence. Dr. Gamaliel, learned and famous teacher of the law, stands up. He cautions them to be careful what they do with these men. He cites two cases on record, two men, Theudas and Judas, who had led popular movements that came to nought. He advised suspended judgment. "If this counsel or this work be of men it will come to nought: but if it be of God, ye cannot overthrow it; lest haply ye be found even to fight against God."

There was a time when I was much impressed with Gamaliel. I thought he made a great speech. It sounded sober, sane and sound, level-headed, reasonable. But the years have changed my convictions about many men, and I have had a radical change of mind about Gamaliel.

The fact is, Gamaliel was an appeaser and he compromised this meeting into a Munich. If Peter was an apostle of Christ, Gamaliel was an apostle of compromise. He was one of the first protagonists of that tolerance which has disgraced the pages of history through the centuries.

There is no excuse for Gamaliel. He was a teacher in Israel and knew these things. He knew the Scriptures about Jesus Christ. And Jesus Christ had come and fulfilled these Scriptures right in Gamaliel's vicinity and in his time, for this thing was not done in a corner. It was no time for suspended judgment. There was nothing to suspend judgment about. Gamaliel should have taken his stand with these apostles. There is a tradition that he became a Christian, but it is more likely that he lived and died a Pharisee. It is to his eternal disgrace that, like Meroz, he came not to the help of the Lord against the mighty. Of course, there would have been a price to pay if he, a teacher in reputation, had taken his stand with these despised Gali-leans. Gamaliel decided to be neither for nor against. He took to the fence, and there he sits as the first of a line of straddlers who have perhaps caused the church more trouble than trouble within or trouble without. God would rather have a man on the wrong side of the fence than *on* the fence. The worst enemies of apostles are not the opposers but the appeasers.

Gamaliel made three mistakes. First, he *made a false comparison.* Although the apostles were immediately in mind, he was really comparing Jesus Christ with Theudas and Judas, for it was Jesus who had started this movement. But you cannot compare Jesus with Theudas or Judas or anybody else. Jesus Christ is Jesus Christ. He admits of no comparison. There is a popular tendency today to airily measure Jesus in the same mold one uses for ordinary men and to compare the Christian movement with man-made religions and enterprises. Some of it has a very scholarly smell and sounds as though it were honest, but it is utterly beside the point. Paul wasted no time compar-ing the Gospel with current religions and trying to convince his hearers that the Gospel was the best answer to the world's ills that had as yet come along. He declared it to be the only answer that ever had come along or ever would come along, all in a class to itself, with all compari-sons out of order. Jesus Christ is Jesus Christ, the first and last. Without Him nothing can be done about salvation. With Him nothing more need be done. Theudas and Judas and all men and movements may be compared with each other but never with Him. God has spoken, God has come, God lived and died and rose again in His Son. That is finality, and all Gamaliels who try to liken something else or someone else to Jesus Christ are trying to compare the incomparable.

Furthermore, Gamaliel *suggested a false criterion.* "We will measure this movement by the success of it. Time will tell." Now, success may be the standard gauge of this world, and "nothing succeeds like success," but earth's yardstick does not apply to Jesus Christ. According to the viewpoint of His time Jesus was a failure. He died in disgrace, the death of a criminal, and His followers were scattered. Nineteen centuries have gone, and today it still looks as though Caesar, not Christ, were on the throne and that the world, the flesh and the devil had things pretty much their way. And, instead of the world being converted, we know that the Lord Himself said, "When the Son of man cometh, shall he find faith on the earth?" That certainly is not success as this world measures it. Nor is it true in the things of Christ that "time will tell." But eternity will tell and we await the verdict of eternity.

The man who postpones taking his stand for Jesus Christ until he sees how the Gospel movement succeeds will live and die with Gamaliel. Visible success has never been the proof of Jesus or His followers. They have been the scum and offscouring of the earth, and although God often blesses true Christians with wealth and advancement in things material, all that is purely incidental. He who tries to use this world's textbooks on success in the things of the Spirit will end up like the man who offered to sell a set of books on "How to Succeed" for a month's room and board! It just doesn't work.

Finally, Gamaliel *arrived at a false conclusion*. "Refrain from these men, and let them alone." But you can't let them alone! You cannot play hands off with the cause of Jesus Christ. "He that is not with me is against me; and he that gathereth not with me scattereth abroad." You cannot suspend judgment and do nothing. You are either dead or alive, and you are either a Christian or you are not. This polite business of waiting to see how it all turns out, adding up all the evidence and making up our minds later when we think all the facts are in, puts man on the pedestal and Jesus before him on trial in the hope of meriting His approval. The fact is, we are guilty and condemned sinners, with the wrath of God abiding on us but with mercy offered, and until we definitely trust Christ we have definitely rejected Him. "He that believeth on him is not condemned: but he that believeth not is condemned already, because he hath not believed in the name of the only begotten Son of God." That admits of no fence-sitters, although many would assume such a position. You cannot leave Jesus Christ or His cause alone. You are with Him or against Him, gathering or scattering, condemned or not condemned.

So Gamaliel was utterly mistaken in what seems at first thought a sound and sane position. He was right when he said that if the Gospel movement were of men it would come to nought but if it were of God it could not be overthrown. But if we get no further than all those "ifs" we shall die in our sins. Until we decide that it is of God and join it, we oppose it. It is we who are on trial. There was a man in a European art gallery who criticized the pictures severely as he walked out the door. The old doorkeeper replied, "If you please, sir, the pictures are no longer on trial but the spectators are!" Christ and the Gospel have proven themselves, and who are we to take the judges' seat and pass on them? God offers salvation as a free gift: take it and you are saved; leave it and you are lost. And until you take it, you leave it.

But Gamaliel's stand reaches out into many applications. As we said at the outset, he was an appeaser, an opportunist, who would not commit himself. We are reminded of the crowd on Carmel when Elijah called down fire from heaven. There were seven thousand in Israel who had not bowed to Baal. There were four hundred and fifty priests of Baal. Both of these groups had at least taken a stand and could be numbered. But when Elijah challenged his congregation, "How long halt ye between two opinions? If the Lord be God, follow him: but if Baal, then follow him," we read that "the people answered him not a word."

They would not commit themselves. They would not take a stand. They would wait and see how things turned out.

This is an age of appeasement. It begins in the home, where the rod is spared and the child spoiled. It continues in school, where right and wrong have become relative instead of absolute. It shows up in nations as it did at Munich. And it has infected the professing church. It does not take a clear stand with Peter and in no uncertain words cut the opposition to the heart. It straddles the fence with Gamaliel and dismisses the assembly.

Erasmus was a typical appeaser, in true succession to Gamaliel. It has been written:

He [Luther] dwells on the ingenious carefulness of Erasmus to avoid decisive utterance, attempting always to shade down his Yes till it is almost a No, and to burnish up his No until it might almost pass for a Yes. Erasmus is a Proteus! He is an eel. . . . In the debate . . . people of academic culture, of speculative disengagement and serene intellectual indifference, sided with Erasmus. The Moderates throughout Europe, the gentlemen of courts, the semi-skeptical intelligences of the universities, told the golden-mouthed apostle of compromise that he was in the right. . . . The heart of Christianity beat with Luther instead.

This is the age of Gamaliel and Erasmus, when, in the name of tolerance, men halt between two opinions and answer not a word. In the church it shows up in Laodicean lukewarmness, a little too hot to be cold and a little too cold to be hot, a state that nauseates the Lord Himself. The Gospel usually makes men mad, sad or glad, but today we walk out of our churches neither sad, mad nor glad—we just walk out. It were better that we went out mad! Gamaliel was neither. Peter was glad in the Lord, and his audience was mad, but Gamaliel was Gamaliel, just tolerant and nothing more.

Such a spirit shows up in our pulpits, where Gamaliels flourish and apostles are few. Joseph Parker, writing about Nathan the prophet, who told King David, "Thou art the man," says:

Definite statements are manageable but vague charges are never to be entertained. He is always a false accuser who makes a general charge; he is a learned false witness skilled and cunning who says he will not go into the case; he will say nothing about it; he thinks it better to hold his tongue. Would God his tongue had been cut when he said that! He has said more by not saying than he could have if he had told the truth. . . . No man makes progress who deals in generalities.

But Nathan belongs to the category of Peter and John and John the Baptist and Paul and Luther—and the Lord of them all. The issue is too clear-cut for middle-of-the-roaders, fundamental modernists and modernistic fundamentalists, neither fish nor fowl. The issues are life and death, heaven and hell, and the case does not call for suspended judgment.

The devil never had a greater ally than this modern atmosphere of genial, amiable, pleasant tolerance, in which nothing is bad, everything is good, and black and white are smeared into an indefinite gray. Nothing matters if everybody is in good humor. Let us not get excited over Peter and John and their Jesus. We will not stoop to take sides. We will see how it works out. Well, the church is still marching on, but nobody ever got anywhere with Gamaliel. Getting mixed up with an unpopular movement is not the worst thing one can do. I would rather have lost my head with James than have kept it with Gamaliel. This modern brand of tolerance has put our age into a stupor. Nothing is important enough to contend for. The devil does great business when the moral sensibilities of men have thus been doped. Even beer ads made much of this "America of kindliness, of friendship, of good-humored tolerance." Well did Gresham Machen say that "the most important things are not those about which men are agreed but those for which men will fight." But the fatigue and languor of this age have got us. Everybody is too dead tired to line up with Peter and the Gospel. It is much more comfortable to suspend judgment and go home to bed.

To be sure, some men have made mistakes on the side of Peter and the Gospel. Peter made some himself. But he never made the supreme mistake of waiting to follow Jesus until he saw how it all turned out. He threw his blundering impetuous self into the Saviour's cause from the very beginning, and although for a while almost everything he said and did was a mistake, his heart was not on the fence. He even denied his Lord, but he came back. The other disciples, too, forsook their Lord and fled. But they ended up, all but Judas, faithful through prison and scourging and martyrdom or lonely exile. They paid the price. Down through the centuries a worthy succession has followed in their train. And along the road they have evermore met their opposers within and without. But the church has never suffered from antagonism half as much as from appeasement. The apostles have had their opposers, but a thousand times more dangerous have been the appeasers.

We can thank God that Gamaliel had one pupil who did not follow in his steps. Paul started out an opposer and ended an apostle, but he never disgraced his name as an appeaser. You could always tell which side of the fence was Paul's. He was on either side with a vengeance. When he was against Christ, he was against Him. When he was for Him, he was for Him. He never sat on the fence with his famous teacher. Paul never could forget that he had opposed the church, but he never had to confess that he appeased the opposition. The opposition slew him, but he outlived it just the same. God help us to follow him as he followed Christ!

GETTING USED TO THE DARK

And have no fellowship with the unfruitful works
of darkness, but rather reprove them

(EPHESIANS 5:11)

SOME TIME AGO a friend of mine took me to a restaurant where they must have loved darkness rather than light. I stumbled into the dimly-lit cavern, fumbled for a chair, and mumbled that I needed a flashlight in order to read the menu. When the food came I ate it by faith and not by sight. Gradually, however, I began to make out objects a little more clearly. My host said, "Funny, isn't it, how we get used to the dark?" "Thank you," I replied, "You have given me a new sermon subject."

We are living in the dark. The closing chapter of this age is dominated by the prince and powers of darkness. Men love darkness rather than light because their deeds are evil. The night is far spent; the blackness is more extensive and more excessive as it deepens just before the dawn. Mammoth Cave is not limited to Kentucky; it is universal!

Strangely enough, man never had more artificial illumination and less true light. Bodily, he walks in unprecedented brilliance, while his soul dwells in unmitigated night. He can release a nuclear glory that outdazzles the sun, and with it he plans his own destruction. He can put satellites in the sky, and left to himself, he is a wandering star to whom is reserved the blackness of darkness forever.

The depths of present-day human depravity are too vile for any word in our language to describe. We are seeing not ordinary moral corruption, but evil double-distilled and compounded in weird, uncanny, and demonic combinations and concoctions of iniquity never heard of a generation ago. This putrefaction of the carcass of civilization awaitng the vultures of judgment is not confirmed to Skid Row; it shows up in the top brackets of society. Plenty of prodigals live morally among swine while garbed in purple and fine linen. A Bishop once said: "There is no difference in reality between the idle rich and the idle poor, between the crowds who loaf in gorgeous hotels and the crowds who tramp the land in rags, save the difference in the cost of their wardrobes and the price of their meals."

Man lives in the dark and even his nuclear flashlight cannot pierce it. We not only live in the dark, we get used to it. There is a slow, subtle, sinister brainwashing process going on and by it we are gradually being desensitized to evil. Little by little, sin is made to appear less sinful until the light within us becomes darkness—and how great is that darkness! Our magazines are loaded with accounts of sordid crime, our newsstands with concentrated corruption. We are engulfed in a tidal wave of pornographic filth. Television has put us in the dark with Sodom and Gomorrah—right in the living room. We get used to it, acclimated to it. We accept, as a matter of course, its art, its literature, its music, its language. We learn to live with it without an inner protest.

Lot was a righteous man, but he moved into Sodom, lived in it, probably became its mayor. His soul was vexed from day to day with the Sodomites' unlawful deeds, but he lost his influence with his family and had to flee for his life. He died in disgrace. I have met many Lots in the past few years! ". . . *as it was in the days of Lot; . . . Even thus shall it be in the day when the Son of*

man is revealed" (LUKE 17:28-30). Modern Lots tell us
that we should hobnob with Sodom and get chummy with
Gomorrah in order to convert them. But the end does
not justify the means. Such people do not turn the light
on in Sodom—they merely get used to the dark.

The worst of all is that such people get so used to
the dark that they think it is growing brighter. Sit long
enough in a dark room and you will imagine that more
light is breaking in. Men who dwell too long in darkness
fancy the day is dawning. We call "broadminded tolerance"
what is really peaceful coexistence with evil. It is an effort
to establish communion between light and darkness, a concord between Christ and Belial.

This condition extends into the religious world and even
into evangelical Christianity. It is possible to fraternize
with unbelievers until false doctrine becomes less and less
objectionable. We come to terms with it and would incor-
porate it into the fellowship of truth. We begin by opening
doors to borderline sects who "believe almost as we do."
Others find overtures from Rome attractive. Still others
would make a crazy quilt of world religions, a syncretism
of "the best in all faiths." "Syncretism" is only a big word
for "hash." These theological chefs who are busy mixing
Mulligan stews think the darkness is lifting; the truth is
that they are merely getting used to it.

The same danger exists with regard to worldliness. One
may live in a twilight zone, in conditions of low visibility,
until he finds the practices of this world less repulsive.
He mistakes the stretching of his conscience for the broad-
ening of his mind. He renounces what he calls the "Phari-
saism" and "puritanism" of earlier days with a good word
for dancing, smoking, and even cocktails now and then.
Instead of passing up Vanity Fair, he spends his vacations
there. John Bunyan tells us that his pilgrims were quite
a novelty to the worldlings: "And as they wondered at
their apparel, so they did likewise at their speech; for few
could understand what they said. They naturally spoke

the language of Canaan; but they that kept the Fair were men of this world. So that from one end of the Fair to the other, they seemed barbarians to each other." How out of date that sounds! Operators of Vanity Fair would see little difference in the clothes, conversation, and conduct of most professing Christians today. If the proprietors of that Fair beheld the modern church member, especially in the summertime, wearing in public a garb in which he should never have left the house or even come downstairs, they would not seem barbarians to each other! Bunyan's pilgrims were not getting used to the dark.

Of course we do not get used to it all of a sudden. Alexander Pope described the gradual process:

> Vice is a monster of such frightful mien,
> As to be hated needs but to be seen;
> Yet seen too oft, familiar with her face,
> We first endure, then pity, then embrace.

Here is how it works. A secular journal says: "The desensitization of 20th-century man is more than a danger to the common safety. . . . *There are some things we have no right ever to get used to.* One . . . is brutality. The other is the irrational. Both . . . have now come together and are moving towards a dominant pattern." There was a time when sin shocked us. But as the brainwashing progresses, what once amazed us only amuses us. We laugh at the shady joke; tragedy becomes comedy; we learn to speak the language of Vanity Fair.

I heard a preacher tell a doubtful joke to a man of this world. Evidently he wanted to give the impression that preachers are used to the dark; actually he was accommodating himself to the dungeon of this age. Dr. John H. Jowett describes this peril of the preacher: "We are tempted to leave our noontide lights behind in our study and to move among men with a dark lantern which we can manipulate to suit our company. We pay the tribute of smiles to the low business standard. We pay the tribute of laughter to the fashionable jest. We pay the tribute of easy tolerance to ambiguous pleasures. We soften everything to a comfortable acquiescence. We seek to be all things to all men to please all. We run with the hare and hunt with the hounds. We become the victims of illicit compromise. There is nothing distinctive about our character." That applies to more people than preachers!

The housewife who moves into suburbia and wants to go along with the group spirit of the community faces the same temptation. So does the organization man at the boss's party or the student on a pagan campus. There are new techniques for socializing at Vanity Fair, but Bunyan's pilgrims had the right idea. We are not here to learn how to live in the dark but to walk in the light. We are not here to get along with evil but to overcome it with good.

One of the signs of getting used to the dark is the way we excuse sin. We give it new names: adultery is free love; the drunkard is an alcoholic; sodomy is homosexuality; the murderer is temporarily insane. Church workers fall into grievous sin and move on to new positions without repentance or change of conduct. Parents let down in discipline, saying, "What's the use?" Pastors give up preaching against sin, arguing that the world's evils are here to stay and since church members are not going to be any better we might as well accept the status quo and live with it. We see this mixture of light and darkness in television programs that join worldliness with hymns. We see it in Hollywood portraying the Bible.

The world lives in the dark because it rejects Jesus Christ, the Light of the world: *"And this is the condemnation, that light is come into the world, and men loved darkness rather than light, because their deeds were evil"* (JOHN 3:19). The word here translated "condemnation" is "crisis" in the original. The coming of Christ precipitated a crisis. It compels men in the very nature of things to come to the light or abide in darkness. This light shines in the Saviour: *"I am the light of the world . . ."* (JOHN 8:12). It shines in the Scriptures: *"Thy word is a lamp unto my feet, and a light unto my path"* (PSALM 119:105). It shines in the saints: *"Ye are the light of the world"* (MATTHEW 5:14). *". . every one that doeth evil hateth the light, neither cometh to the light, lest his deeds should be reproved"* (JOHN 3:20). That explains why some people do not come to church.

I remember a couple in my first pastorate. The husband, an unsaved man, brought his wife to church on Sunday nights, but he sat outside in his car. He was in the dark in more ways than one because he did not like to face the gospel light. His wife enjoyed the service because she loved the light and came to the light that her deeds might be made manifest that they were wrought in God. When you overturn a stone in the field and the sunlight strikes beneath it, all the hidden creeping and crawling things scurry for cover. So do our sinful hearts grow restless under the light of God's truth. In an unlighted cellar you do not see the spiders and snakes and lizards and toads until the light breaks in. So men do not realize their sinfulness until they face the Light. No wonder some live in the dark all week and then blink their eyes and wince in church on Sunday morning when the preacher turns on the Light! They have photophobia—they fear the Light.

Our business as Christians is to let our light shine: *". . . have no fellowship with the unfruitful works of darkness, but rather reprove [expose, turn the light on] them"* (EPHESIANS 5:11). We expose them not so much by denunciation, although that has its place, but by the contrast of our godly living. Alas, we are so afraid of being offensive that we are not effective! Our Lord said that two things would smother the light of our testimony, a bushel and a bed. Today we dim our light in a third way: we turn it low for fear of creating a disturbance;

we shade it to match the dim dungeon of this age. We would rather grieve the Holy Spirit than offend the wicked.

The early Christians did not dim their lights to match the times. Paul exceedingly troubled the places he visited, and even in prison at midnight he turned night into day. The saints in Rome lighted the streets with their burning bodies. Christians met in catacombs, but they illuminated the world.

We are a city set on a hill, not hidden in a dungeon. We are to shine as lights in the world. This is no time to get used to the dark; it is time to turn on the Light! Too long have the caverns of this world been undisturbed. Of course some cave dwellers will squirm, but others will see our good works and glorify our Father in heaven. Light has no communion with darkness. We are not here to commune with it but to conquer it, and *"this is the victory that overcometh the world, even our faith"* (I JOHN 5:4).

Early Christianity set the world aglow because absolute Light was pitched against absolute darkness. The early Christians believed that the gospel was the only hope of the world, that without it all men were lost and all religions false. The day came when the church and the world mixed light and darkness. The church got used to the dark and lived in it for several centuries, with only occasional flashes of light. Today too many Christians think there is some darkness in our light and some light in the world's darkness. We half-doubt our own gospel and half-believe the religion of this age. We are creeping around in the dark when we should be flooding the world with light. We need to get our candles out from under bushels and beds, take off the shades of compromise and let them shine in our hearts, our homes, our businesses, our churches, and our communities with that light that shines in the Saviour and in the Scriptures and in the saints.

HAVE YOU LOST THE WONDER?

*And said, Verily I say unto you, except ye be convert-
ed; and become as little children, ye shall not enter
into the kingdom of heaven* (MATTHEW 18:3)

GYPSY SMITH, the great evangelist, died on a journey
in true Gypsy tradition in his eighty-seventh year. Called
to preach at seventeen, he was simple and original and
colorful. He said, "I was born in a field; don't put me in a
flowerpot." He was not a theologian; he would have agreed
with Sam Jones, who said he liked flowers but not botany,
religion but not theology. He was in a class with Billy
Sunday, who used to say that he didn't know any more
about theology than did a jack rabbit about ping-pong.
When he was advised to learn how to sing from his diaphragm, Gypsy replied that he didn't want to sing from his
diaphragm but from his heart.

When asked about the secret of his freshness and vigor,
even into old age, he said, *"I have never lost the wonder."*
A preacher should have the mind of a scholar, the heart
of a child, and the hide of a rhinoceros. His biggest problem is how to toughen his hide without hardening his
heart. Gypsy Smith had the heart of a child. He never
lost the wonder.

Is not this one thing our Lord meant when He said,
"Except ye be converted; and become as little children,

ye shall not enter into the kingdom of heaven" (MATTHEW 18:3)? Children have not lost the wonder. They have not been here long enough to get used to it. They still have a sense of surprise—anything may happen, everything is new. At five they have all the questions, and at eighteen they know all the answers. With a child, every turn of the road may hold a glad discovery. The commonest, most humdrum day is glorified by the glamour of imagination, for life is one-fourth fact and three-fourths fancy.

All too soon, and sooner now than ever, children lose the wonder. A popular magazine inquired recently, "What happened to the Magic of Childhood?" Youngsters become cynical, fed-up, sophisticated before they reach their teens. In a television age they have already seen everything. What could possibly surprise them? Recently, in a Mennonite settlement, I read this motto: "We are too soon oldt and too late schmart." "Too smart too soon" would describe the plight of modern youth.

Youth is not entirely to blame. Oldsters have no time to wonder, to reflect, to meditate about anything. We must always be "doing something." There is no time to walk in the woods, to sit before an open fire, "just thinking." Everything is organized, supervised, planned, programmed, and correlated. We don't walk—we take organized hikes. We don't wander along, watching birds—we join a club and keep records. We lose the wonder of it in the work of it.

This gets into Christian experience. What should be a life of faith working by love becomes high-pressure "religious activity." What should be a Thessalonian work of faith and a labor of love and a patience of hope becomes just Ephesian work and labor and patience.

We lose the wonder because too many Christains become childish instead of childlike. They are spiritual babies who won't grow up; milk-feeders who should be on meat; carnal believers, not newborn babes desiring the sincere milk of the Word; overgrown babies who keep pastors busy with a milk bottle. We are not to be "children, tossed to and fro, and carried about with every wind of doctrine, by the sleight of men, and cunning craftiness, whereby they lie in wait to deceive; But speaking the truth in love, [we] may grow up into him in all things, which is the head, even Christ" (EPHESIANS 4:14-15). We ought to grow up and out of childishness into childlikeness. This secret is kept from the wise and prudent and revealed unto babes. There is not so much to learn as to unlearn. A revival comes when childish church members become childlike in simple faith and obedience.

A childlike Christian does not lose the wonder. There ought to be in every child of God a sense of surprise, a glad expectancy. This is his Father's world and anything can happen. We live on a miracle level and faith is not believing that God *can,* but that He *will* do wonderful things. But we do not look for miracles, and we do not see many. We pray for rain, and do not carry our umbrellas. We ought never to start for a meeting without saying, "This may be the great night!" We get used to being Christians; we take it for granted and we lose the wonder. We work at it harder than ever, but we are shorn Samsons in treadmills. "Christian activity" becomes a battle of wits and a bustle of works. Nothing else under the sun can be as dry, flat, tedious, and exhausting as religious work without the wonder. We dread going to church. We are bored by the sermon. The Sunday-school lesson puts us to sleep. Church visiting is drudgery and singing in choir a chore. We are weary in well-doing. Once we stood amazed in the presence of Jesus the Nazarene; now we want to sit amused. Once we were edified; now we must be entertained. It is all work and no wonder.

A passenger on a long train trip was so enthralled by the journey that every few moments he was heard to say, "Wonderful!" The passing scenery, the faces of the fellow passengers, even the smallest details elicited from him glad expressions of keen enjoyment. Finally one traveler, overcome by curiosity, asked him, "How is it that while the rest of us are worn out with this monotonous trip, you are having the time of your life and you keep saying, " 'Wonderful!' " He answered, "Until a few days ago, I was a blind man. A great doctor has just given me my sight and what is ordinary to the rest of you is 'out of this world' to me."

If the Great Physician has opened our eyes; if we have been to Siloam's Pool and have come back seeing, if we have had the touch by which we no longer see men as trees walking—if all that has happened to us, why shouldn't we make our way through this poor world singing?

Wonderful, wonderful, Jesus is to me,
Prince of Peace, Counsellor, Mighty God is He;
Saving me and keeping me from all sin and shame,
He is my Redeemer, praise His Name!

RESIGNED OR RE-SIGNED?

Then I said, I will not make mention of him, nor speak any more in his name. But his word was in mine heart as a burning fire shut up in my bones, and I was weary with forbearing, and I could not stay (JEREMIAH 20:9)

IN THIS REMARKABLE verse the prophet Jeremiah announces the impossible; he resigns and then declares immediately that he cannot resign; he quits but he cannot quit. Any true preacher can understand Jeremiah's crisis. Almost every man of God has had a spell when he was ready to resign, and knew all the time that he couldn't. A man cannot really preach until preach he must. If he can do something else, he probably should! Paul said, ". . . *woe is unto me, if I preach not the gospel!*" (I CORINTHIANS 9:16). Necessity was laid upon him; he had to do it.

Becoming a minister is not a matter of looking over an assortment of professions—law, medicine, physics, music—and then saying, "I think I'll be a preacher." God is not running a cafeteria where you choose your favorite piece of pie. Jeremiah had a holy bone-fire. He did not merely have to say something—he had something to say. There is a lot of difference between pouring out one's heart and getting something off one's chest. Many a preacher has spent an hour in the pulpit airing his pet grievances under the impression that he was speaking for God.

95

Such men are ready to resign when things don't go their way. A preacher who runs a heavenly fever like Jeremiah's cannot resign, even though nothing goes his way.

We are hearing a lot about how hard it is to be a Christian in these perilous times. We sigh for "the good old days" and paint around them a brighter halo than they deserve. *"Say not thou, What is the cause that the former days were better than these? for thou dost not enquire wisely concerning this"* (ECCLESIASTES 7:10). A subscriber complained to a magazine editor, "Your magazine is not as good as it used to be." The editor replied, "It never has been." When we look at former times, "distance lends enchantment to the view." When was it ever easy to be a Christian? The times have never been propitious. Dr. Phillips says, "Many Christians talk about the difficulties of the times as though we should have to wait for better ones before the Christian religion can take root. It is heartening to remember that this faith took root and flourished amazingly in conditions that would have killed anything less vital in a matter of weeks."

And yet it is true that, as the age draws near to its close, evil is intensified. The devil has pulled out all the stops and stepped up the pressure. But this world is not our rest; it is a training ground for Christian character. You cannot sharpen an axe on a pound of butter.

What is the best way to face this insane age and make our way through this madhouse without going crazy in it? What is a preacher to do when he faces exhaustion in this rat-race? What is he to do when, as Woodrow Wilson once put it, he has worn out his constitution and is living on his by-laws? How is he to carry on in a day when he is a back number if he does not have to his credit (or discredit) one ulcer, one heart attack, or one nervous breakdown?

He can resign. Jeremiah must have had some such inclination when he wrote, *"Oh that I had in the wilderness a lodging place of wayfaring men; that I might leave my*

people, and go from them!" (9:2). He is not the only
preacher who has felt like leaving his pulpit to go into
the motel business! After all, couldn't he serve the Lord
there, testifying to the tourists and giving his money to
good causes! At any rate, some have tried such moves
and always to their sorrow. Some do their own resigning;
others are spared the trouble! Some spend five years resigning while others leave overnight, as though jet-propelled.

There is not much information available on why some
preachers quit. One could stock a library with reports of
miracles that happened "since I came." They sound like
Jonah reporting his campaign in Nineveh. But I have never
read much on "why I left." Some leave because they are
"Cape Kennedy pastors," using their present pulpits as
platforms from which to blast satellites into bigger orbits.
Others are simply discouraged, like Matthew Henry who
thought his ministry was a failure—and yet he lives on
in book shelves and in our hearts today. Some sink into
self-pity and lament that they are not appreciated. Blessed
is the man who learns quite early that the ministry is
the poorest business in the world if one is looking merely
for appreciation! After all, a preacher is not to be measured
by how many bouquets have been given to him. His ministry may be gauged better by how many brickbats have
been pitched at him. Prophets of God have usually been
on the receiving end of more mud than medals.

The most miserable men I have known are ministers
who have turned in their commissions. Anybody can quit.
The church is plagued with quitters, who say, "I go, sir,"
and go not; who received the Word with joy but have
no root and are soon offended. Many sing in the choir
for a few weeks and then their feelings are hurt and the
nightingale becomes a raven croaking, "Nevermore!" Others come to church for months, and then golf becomes
more important than God. Others are church officers until
they find out that they cannot run the place, and then
they resign because they would rather be Diotrephes loving

the preeminence than Demetrius loving the truth. But sad-
dest of all is the preacher who quits preaching. No reward
on earth can compensate for that. To be a faithful preacher
is no bed of roses, but for a God-called man to become
anything else is to try to rest his soul on a bed of thorns.
No, the way out is not by resigning.

There is a second possibility for the discouraged minister: *he can become resigned.* He can accept the status
quo and go along with it, taking the line of least resistance.
Some things are *inevitable,* and a man must face them,
even then not with mere resignation because he cannot
help himself or with mere submission, but with acceptance,
saying with bowed head, "Thy will be done." But there
are two ways of saying, "Thy will be done." Some things
are not God's will. They are not to be accepted with bowed
head in meek resignation. They are wrong and should be
changed, and we should face them with heads erect, saying,
"Thy will be done—and I'll do my part to see that it
is done."

Should we resign ourselves to things as they are and
bring our preaching down to suit a generation that cannot
endure sound doctrine—all because we have grown weary
of holding up a standard to which they do not intend
to conform? The worst thing a preacher can do is retreat
to his outfit because it refuses to catch up with the standard.
Of course it is lonely business out in front. Such a man
becomes a target and may be shot at by either the enemy
in front or his own regiment behind him.

Life has its inevitables and they are to be met with
calm acceptance. It has it impossibles and they are to
be faced with common sense. But it also has its inexcus-
ables and they are not to be tolerated with resignation.
The early Christians did not adjust to the situation; they
adjusted the situation! Martin Luther did not say, "I don't
like the way things are going, but I'm not sticking my
neck out." John Wesley did not say, "I deplore the deadness
of the church, but what can I do about it? I'm not risking

my bread and butter on nonconformity." Our forefathers did not resign and quit; neither did they become resigned to the status quo of their day. One thing is certain: they did not trot out that alibi so popular now, "Oh, well, we might as well accept it—these things are here to stay." Of course some conditions are here to stay to the end of the age. So is the devil, so is sin. Liquor is probably here to stay; people are going to drink it and make it and sell it, but that does not excuse legalizing it. Immorality is here to stay, but that is no alibi for making it respectable. *". . . evil men . . . shall wax worse and worse . . ."* (II TIMOTHY 3:13), but that is no justification for coddling criminals and growing sentimental about delinquency. Dancing is here to stay, but that does not mean we must bring it into the church. Television is here to stay, but we need not let it flood our homes with filth because we are too lazy to supervise what we see or let others see.

We live in a day of resignation, not to the inevitable, but to the inexcusable and unjustifiable. In the international realm we are resigned to communism with our policy of appeasement, compromise, and peaceful coexistence in hopeless toleration of what should have been isolated and quarantined like smallpox. "Communism is here to stay" —is the argument—"so let's recognize Red China." In the church we have adopted a similar policy of accommodation: "Let us accept things as they are and go along with the status quo. The end justifies the means." The Church at Corinth accepted the immorality of one of its members and was resigned to it. The church at Pergamos tolerated Balaamism, and Thyatira "suffered that woman Jezebel." Our Lord judges us in what we put up with as much as in what we actively practice. The minister therefore cannot resign himself to a situation when God wants him to change it or at least speak for God to the situation.

If the preacher is not to resign or become resigned,

there is another thing he can do: *he can be re-signed*. Was it not a great preacher of the past who, in this discouragement, offered to resign only to receive from the Lord this impression: "What you need is not to resign your commission, but to have your commission re-signed!"

Dr. C. I. Scofield tells us that in all the years he was associated with D. L. Moody, the great evangelist rarely prayed with him without asking God to renew Scofield's commission. "That petition always gave me food for thought, and sometimes anxious thought," he says. "Was it indeed true that I was going on in my ministry under an expired commission? Or, if matters were not at that sad pass, had the signature of my Master upon it grown dim?"

Dr. Scofield goes on: "In company with a good Welsh brother, I was once listening to a sermon on the healing of Naaman. It was a good sermon from a homiletical standpoint, and I admitted it to myself in a kind of protest against an inner feeling that somehow, good as it was, it was leaving me cold. Just then my friend leaned over and sighed, 'If only the dear brother would take a fresh dip in Jordan himself!' When the sermon was ended, *my* message had come from the Welsh brother. I walked away into the night, I know not whither, for death seemed in my heart, and I kept my face to the stars as I tried to tell God that I was the 'dear man' who needed that fresh dip in Jordan."

I used to think that it was only ministers who had fallen into grievous sin who needed a fresh dip in Jordan; but if I read my Bible aright, some of God's men had their commissions re-signed in the midst of an active ministry. Joshua met the Captain of the Lord of Hosts when he was already the leader of his people. Isaiah had his lips touched with fire when he was already a prophet crying, "Woe is this!" and "Woe is that!"—he needed to get around to "Woe is me!" Daniel was man enough to turn down a king's table and spend a night in a lion's den rather than deny God; but he still needed an experience when his comeliness turned to corruption. Job had set an example of fortitude and faithfulness to God in the midst of unparalleled adversity; but he still needed to come to the day when he could say, *"I have heard of thee by the hearing of the ear: but now mine eye seeth thee"* (42:5). None of us begins to compare with these men even *before* they had their commissions re-signed.

Many a minister needs such an experience when he is successful, prosperous, and popular, living in a whirl of activity with his church finances in good shape and himself among the top men in the synagogue. For all of that, the signature of God on his credentials may be growing dim. Leaving first love and then losing the joy of salvation may take place in the midst of what passes for a successful ministry. It is almost impossible to get at such a man and convince him of his plight. He may resent the suggestion. And if he should suspect his true condition, how and when can he be still long enough to get his commission re-signed? There are substitutes: a post-graduate course (when he may already have more degrees than temperature!); a trip to Palestine; and ecclesiastical promotion. But these are only Abana and Pharpar, rivers of Damascus, when a man needs a fresh dip in Jordan.

D. L. Moody was in the midst of a most successful ministry when two old ladies kept praying that he might have a renewed commission—and he did! A book that helped me greatly at a turning-point in my life, *Deeper Experiences of Famous Christians*, is a long record of re-signed credentials, men of God who came to a fresh dip in Jordan; and the amazing thing is that most of them were doing well, by ordinary standards, before their renewal. The average preacher today would be glad to settle for what most of them had *before* they moved out of their good into God's best.

One reason why we are satisfied with less these days is because most churches are. How many pulpit committees do you know who put first in their requirements for a new minister: "Does he know God? Is the Divine signature fresh upon him?" A lot of churches do not want a Jeremiah with the fire of God in his bones. He might make them too uncomfortable every Sunday!

Another angle does not even enter into our thinking any more. If a preacher should have a new experience with God, that does not necessarily mean that he would go up another rung on the ladder of success. In some quarters he might be demoted! It might mean loss of station, loss of honors, loss of friends. That is utterly foreign to our thinking these days when the positive thinkers are telling us that if we affirm our faith three times before breakfast, we shall be president of the company before we are forty. Plenty of congregations would not welcome the information if the pastor should have his commission renewed. In some situations, if a minister went all the way to his Lord without the camp bearing His reproach, it might be his last Sunday in that pulpit. A deeper experience of God is no guarantee of a call to a bigger church. A man had better not ask God to restamp his preaching orders these days with the idea that it will enhance his reputation and insure his succession. He had better be prepared to lose his reputation and forego his success, for "as the Master, so must the servant be." Never forget that John was on Patmos for ". . . *the word of God, and . . . the testimony of Jesus Christ . . .*" (REVELATION 1:2). But, after all, Patmos was a promotion, for it gave us the Revelation!

One thing is certain: a minister may have his study walls lined with diplomas, his ordination papers signed by illustrious men, a sheaf of recommendations from the mighty of the land, but if the stamp of heaven on his commission is faint and fading, he had better close up shop and take time out until he can return to his pulpit with a brand-new autograph from God. When he is thus re-signed, he will be reassigned, like Elijah, like Jonah, like Peter. He may be given the same task, for some churches need not a new preacher, but the same preacher renewed. Whatever the task, old or new, he is ready for anything because he is fresh from the Main Office. And he is equipped to serve out his earthly apprenticeship until that day when *"his servants shall serve him: And they shall see his face; and his name shall be in their foreheads"* (REVELATION 22:3-4). That is the final and eternal autograph—and it will never fade!

THE FOUR-HUNDRED-AND-FIRST PROPHET

*Is there not here a prophet of the Lord besides,
that we might enquire of him?* (I KINGS 22:7)

THERE IS NO period of Bible history more dramatic than
the life and times of Ahab. Some of the worst and some
of the best Old Testament characters were his contemporaries. There was Jezebel, one of the wickedest women
who ever lived, and there was Elijah, who lived in a tempest
and went to heaven in a whirlwind. The times were evil
but they were not dull. Something was happening every
minute.

On one occasion, Ahab planned a campaign against
Ramoth-gilead. It was a case of a bad man doing a good
thing in the wrong way. He had Scripture for the undertak-
ing (DEUTERONOMY 4:43), but it takes more than a verse
to justify such a venture. Ahab inveigled King Jehoshaphat
of Judah into joining him in the enterprise. Jehoshaphat
was a good man but easily influenced. Ahab put on a
banquet—a kick-off supper is usually all it takes to line
up a Jehoshaphat. The King of Judah had no business
in such a project, and the prophet Jehu asked him, *"Shouldest thou help the ungodly, and love them that hate the
Lord?"* (II CHRONICLES 19:2). That text ought to be
brought out of the moth balls and put into circulation!

Jehoshaphat asked that the Israelites enquire of the Lord.

104

It was a little late, since they had already made up their minds, but four hundred false prophets were called in and they were unanimous in their opinion. When four hundred preachers agree, there may be grounds for suspicion. Jehoshaphat asked, "Is there not here a prophet of the Lord *besides,* that we may enquire of him?" Give him credit at least for raising the issue: *"Isn't there somebody around who speaks for God?"* Ahab replied, *"There is yet one man . . ."* (I KINGS 19:8). Thank God, there usually is! Ahab added, ". . . but I hate him"—which is to the eternal credit of that one man—"because he doth not prophesy good concerning me, but evil" (verse 8). Does that not remind us of the Greatest Prophet of all, who said, *". . . me it [the world] hateth, because I testify of it, that the works thereof are evil"* (JOHN 7:7)?

While a messenger went to bring Micaiah, one of the false prophets put a theatrical touch on his prophecy and added a dash of Hollywood. Zedekiah waved horns and dramatized the success of the forthcoming venture. It is bad enough to be a false prophet, but to be a ham actor besides is too much.

It was a day of unification, with Ahab and Jehoshaphat uniting; it was a day of *unanimity,* with four hundred prophets in unison; it was a day of *uniformity.* The messenger advised Micaiah that the clergy had agreed and that he should go along with them. But Micaiah had not been regimented, standardized, collectivized, or brainwashed. He had no axe to grind. He was not riding the bandwagon. He was not on his way up. The grass did not look greener in the next pasture and he craved no man's bishopric. He was not a link in anybody's chain.

Joseph Parker said, "The world hates the four-hundred-and-first prophet." Micaiah was Number 401. He broke the monotony when he said, *"As the Lord liveth, what the Lord saith unto me, that will I speak"* (I KINGS 22:14). He was put on a diet of bread and water, but better a prophet on bread and water than a politician at the feasts of Ahab. With his immortal words Micaiah answered the question of Jehoshaphat: he was the prophet of the Lord *besides*.

We live in days not unlike the times of Micaiah. It is a time of *unification*. Ahab and Jehoshaphat are still going up against Ramoth-gilead. The world is being unified into the world state, the churches into the world church. It is a time of *unanimity*, of yes-men and rubber stamps. Adlai Stevenson is reported to have said that he had devised a new word, "yo," which can mean either "yes" or "no"! It is a time of *uniformity*. We are like eggs in a crate. We talk about being "different" but never have we been more alike. Teen-agers boast of being different but they dress alike, talk alike, look alike. The human race is gradually being homogenized into one faceless, monolithic mass. It is the day of the lowest common denominator, the happy medium, the middle of the road. A pleasant "get-alongism," a "togetherness," has so paralyzed us into moral inertia that it is almost impossible to arouse us from our amiable stupor. The steamroller is flattening all the mountains into one level plain. Such a time does not breed prophets.

Men who speak for God never merge into the fog around them. Noah stood alone in a civilization of culture and progress. His contemporaries must have laughed at him as an eccentric who was building an oversized houseboat and looking for the world to end. Elijah stood alone among the priests of Baal and the stooges who ate at Jezebel's table. When he challenged the multitude, that fifth-amendment crowd "answered not a word." Amos stood alone in the religio-political system of his day. Dr. Kyle Yates wrote, "His time had not been spent in a divinity school. He was unwilling to be classed as a member of the guilds who made their living by bowing to the wishes of the people and preaching a pleasing message that would guarantee a return engagement." Jeremiah stood alone among the tranquilizers of his day who were preaching peace when there was no peace; but we are still reading Jeremiah while the happiness boys of his day have been forgotten. Daniel spoke for God in the midst of a pagan empire and it was worth a night in a lion's den to be able to read God's handwriting on the wall. Paul conferred not with flesh and blood but got his orders direct from Headquarters. He was not the product of any assembly line. Dr. Mordecai Ham said, "Paul was a strategist who thought out his strategy on the field of war, not in some Jerusalem war office where parchment and sealing wax were more plentiful than experience and foresight."

True prophets are solitary people; eagles do not fly in flocks. It is not easy to be a Lone Dissenter. When the messenger was sent for Micaiah he must have said, in effect, "The clergy have agreed, and you had better make it unanimous. It is quite an honor to speak before two kings and four hundred prophets. What is it getting you to be an odd number? This is a good gravy train and you had better ride it. This is the mood of the hour and you had better get with it." The same subtle pressure today would persuade preachers to get in step with the times and ride the wave of the future. What we need are more preachers out of step with the times, more odd prophets like Micaiah. We are told that we must adjust. Adjust to what? What is there in this world set-up to adjust to? God's man needs to adjust only to God's Word and God's will. It is not the business of the prophet to harmonize with the times. "... *what concord hath Christ with Belial?*" (II CORINTHIANS 6:15). The preacher is a soloist; he was never meant to play the accompaniment to anything. The pulpit is not a platform from which to boost the projects of men to bring in a false millennium, the Kingdom without the King. No matter how much Scripture may be quoted or how many false prophets bid Ahab go up against Ramoth-gilead, Micaiah will stand his ground and refuse to be swept off his feet by popular movements. The greatest need of the hour is a four-hundred-and-first prophet of the Lord *besides*, that we may enquire of him.

There are several ways of silencing a prophet. *Persecution* will do it. John the Baptist's head is not always brought in on a charger; there are newer ways of decapitating the prophet with more finesse. *Promotion* sometimes does it. The prophet is given a high seat in the synagogue and is never heard from again. The *pressure* of the times and discouragement can do it. Jeremiah wanted to quit preaching, get out in the wilderness, and run a motel. *Another prophet* can sometimes do it, as when the prophet at Bethel backslid in his own revival, and he who could turn down a king was deceived by another prophet.

Prophets are not popular at home; they are without honor in their own countries. They are not popular with politicians. Ahab hated Micaiah—but he feared him enough to disguise himself when he went to battle, lest Micaiah's predictions came true. There was another prophet by the name of Obadiah who was out with Ahab looking for grass when he should have been with Elijah praying for rain. The true prophet does not know how to work both sides of the street. He refuses to dine with Jeroboam and does not let his hair down with the priests of Bethel.

Prophets are not popular with Pharisees. Our Lord asked, *"Which of the prophets have not your fathers persecuted?"* (ACTS 7:52), and He said, *". . . ye are the children of them that killed the prophets"* (MATTHEW 23:31). One generation stones prophets and the next builds sepulchers in their honor.

> Seven wealthy towns contend for Homer dead,
> Through which the living Homer begged his bread.

Joseph Parker said, "There are those today who would clap their hands at the name of Bunyan who would not admit a living Bunyan to fellowship." Organized religion hates the preacher whose headquarters is heaven, whose Superintendent is God. They are enraged when they cannot control him. The times are never propitious for the Lone Dissenter.

Naturally, one can hardly expect a sermon on Micaiah to be any more popular than its subject. But it is worth preaching if in the congregation one man will hear and heed the call to be a New Testament prophet. If such a prospect is reading this, God bless you. The odds will be four hundred to one, the diet may be bread and water, and the orders are: ". . . what the Lord saith unto me, that will I speak." If you are interested in the prophetic ministry, get ready for trouble! You will be despised by Amaziah and all who want to preserve the status quo at Bethel. You will be hated by Jezebel and all who would set up the worship of Baal alongside the altar of Jehovah. You will be too angular to fit the Procrustean beds of the religious world. You will not be able to feather your nest in this world; scant provision is made for prophets down here. You will report to Heavenly Headquarters and get your orders from the Main Office. If you are a prospect, think it over. You had better mean business, else your ministry will be pathetic instead of prophetic. And remember that prophets are needed but not wanted.

It is time for another four-hundred-and-first prophet of the Lord *besides*, that we might enquire of him.

THE CHRISTIAN AND THIS WORLD

SERMONS ON WORLDLINESS are rare these days. The new word is "secularism." Billy Sunday used to say that the term "worldly Christian" was a misnomer. Of course, Billy didn't put it that way. He said, "You might as well talk about a heavenly devil!" That is in line with the New Testament definition that the friend of the world is the enemy of God.

I am convinced that many people we call worldly Christians are not Christians at all. Our Saviour said, *"My sheep hear my voice . . . and they follow me"* (JOHN 10:27). A sheep may fall into a mudhole but is not satisfied to stay there. A hog is at home in a mudhole, and Peter tells us that false teachers who revert to their evil ways belong in that category.

It is true that we are not to judge people. *"The Lord knoweth them that are his"* (II TIMOTHY 2:19), and I am glad that He does, otherwise some of them would be pretty hard to identify! That same verse goes on to declare that all who claim to be the Lord's should depart from iniquity. When I see a bird that talks like a duck, quacks like a duck, paddles in the water like a duck, and prefers the company of ducks, I conclude that it must be a duck. "Birds of a feather flock together," and where we feel most at home is where we belong. *"We know that we have passed from death unto life, because we love the brethren,"* (JOHN 3:14). If we do not enjoy being with the

110

brethren, certain conclusions are in order. When Peter and John were let go, we read that they went to their own company. Where do you go when you are let go? I'd hate to track down some church members when they get several hundred miles away from home. When Peter got out of jail, he headed for a prayer meeting. We gravitate to what lures us most and eventually show up where, at heart, we belong.

The world that God so loved that He gave His Son is the world of lost souls, and we ought to love lost souls. It was Dr. Candlish who said: "If we loved this world as God loved it we would not love it as we shouldn't love it." When God's Word says, *"Love not the world . . ."* (JOHN 2:15), it means this present age and set-up which is under the devil, the god of this age, and the prince of this world. The whole world lies in wickedness. Our Lord came to deliver us from this present evil world (GALATIANS 3:4). Before we were saved, we walked according to the course of this world. (EPHESIANS 2:2), but after we are saved we head in another direction.

John has more to say about the world than any other New Testament writer. In our Lord's high, priestly prayer, in the seventeenth chapter of John, He forever locates us as believers with regard to this age. First, He says we have been saved *out of the world* (v. 6). We are the called-out ones. We have been saved out of this world system and given a new position with Christ in the heavenlies. Our citizenship is in heaven, and our standing up there and our state down here, our position up there and our condition down here ought to match. We are pilgrims and strangers, exiles and aliens, and this world is our passage but not our portion, as Matthew Henry said long ago. The Scriptures tell us, ". . . *this is not your rest*" (MICAH 2:10), and ". . . *here have we no continuing city . . ."* (HEBREWS 13:14). A dog is at home in this world for this is the only world a dog will ever know, but we cannot make ourselves at home here for we were made for another world.

Our Lord said furthermore that we are *in the world* (verse 11). Although we have been saved out of it, we still have to live in its houses, trade in its stores, and mix with its people. The old mystics tried to make themselves holier by hiding from society, but living in a hole does not make you holier! Indeed, Paul wrote that to avoid companying with evil men, we would have to leave this world (I CORINTHIANS 5:10). Our Lord prayed in this same high priestly prayer: *"I pray not that thou shouldest take them out of the world, but that thou shouldest keep them from the evil"* (verse 15). He was in the world, and was not a recluse nor a hermit. He went to weddings, and was called a friend of publicans and sinners. Where cross the crowded ways of men, He could be found. He was criticized by the Pharisees who were separated from sinners but not from sin. He associated with the world, but had no fellowship with it.

He says further, *they are not of the world* (verses 14,16). This is so important that He repeats it. When the boat is in the water, that is one matter; when the water is in the boat, that is something else. We are not to be conformed to this world (ROMANS 12:2); we are to keep ourselves unspotted from the world (JAMES 1:27); we are to have no fellowship with the unfruitful works of darkness (EPHESIANS 5:11). We are not to love the world, neither the things that are in the world (I JOHN 2:15). We are to deny ungodliness and the lusts of this age (TITUS 2:12). This imposing world set-up with its pagan culture, is no friend of grace to help us on to God. We cannot serve two masters. Alexander McLaren said: "The measure of our discord with the world is the measure of our accord with Christ." Gypsy Smith said: "If you are in with God, you are at outs with this world." Dr. G. Campbell Morgan said: "The world hates Christian people, that is, if they see Christ in them. The measure in which the world agrees with us and says we are really a fine type of Christian, we are so entirely broad, is the measure in which we are unlike Christ."

Our Lord said to His brothers: "The world cannot hate you; but me it hateth, because I testify of it, that the works thereof are evil" (JOHN 7:7). He said to His disciples: *"If the world hate you, ye know that it hated me before it hated you. If ye were of the world, the world would love his own: but because ye are not of the world, but I have chosen you out of the world, therefore the world hateth you"* (JOHN 15:18,19). Put all of this together and we have this: the world cannot hate its own, but it hates Jesus Christ and will hate His true disciples. *". . . the world knoweth us not, because it knew him not"* (I JOHN 3:1). All of these verses from JOHN ought to settle forever the status of the Christian in this world.

The Saviour said one thing more in His prayer concerning this matter: *"As Thou hast sent me into the world, even so have I also sent them into the world"* (verse 18). Here, then, is the summing up of the Christians relation to this world as set forth in our Lord's prayer. We have been saved *out of the world*; we still must live *in the world*; we are not *of the world*; we have been saved to go back *into the world* to win others out of it, and that is the only business we have in the world! We are not to sit in judgment on the age. We are the salt of the earth and the light of the world, and, as our Lord said in this same prayer (verse 19) for their sakes we should sanctify ourselves—be set apart—to minister to the need of this age.

The Way of the Cross Leads Home is a familiar old song. Everybody would agree to the first verse, that there is no other way, but we are not so agreed on the last verse:

Then I bid farewell to the way of the world,
to walk in it nevermore.

It is quite evident that we cannot walk two ways at once. There is only one song for the Christian on this point:

> The world behind me, the cross before me,
> No turning back, no turning back.

THOSE CHOICE SPIRITS

ANDREW MURRAY, the great Christian leader and writer of South Africa, was deeply interested in faith healing for some years. His biographer tells us, however, that during the latter part of his life, Dr. Murray came to the conclusion that faith healing was not for everyone but only for "those choice spirits who are so simple and steadfast in faith, and so completely detached from the world, as to be able sincerely and unreservedly to place themselves in God's hands."

I am not now concerned with the subject of faith healing but rather with this description of that comparative few in every generation, here designated as "choice spirits." The writer does not mean a clique of super-saints. He does not have in mind certain favorites of the Almighty who can claim blessings denied to run-of-the-mill Christians. He is not suggesting that there are rarefied spiritual heights accessible only to a select minority while the rest of us plug along in the valleys below. He does not intimate that only a handful *can* climb to the altitudes but he does declare, and rightly, that only a few ever *do*.

The number of "choice spirits" is not legion. They are not necessarily scholars, although one could be both. They are not usually celebrities, for many are obscure and lowly in their church and community. They are often quiet souls of modest means and station, but they have learned a secret theologians sometimes miss. To discover that secret, there is not so much to learn as to unlearn. Most of us know too much. We have read too many books and heard too many experts. We cannot get low enough to be convert-ed and become as little children. When our Lord was on earth, scribes and Pharisees who knew the Scriptures missed His blessing while poor, sick and sinful souls pressed into the Kingdom. Many a dignified religionist in the crowds that followed Jesus never once got the idea, while Bartimaeus got his sight and Zacchaeus salvation and a poor woman, with health and money gone, touched Him and was made whole.

We are told that choice spirits have a simple and stead-fast faith, are completely detached from the world and able sincerely and unreservedly to place themselves in God's hands. These are well-worn phrases in some circles but how many ever meet that test? Dr. Murray felt that such people are healed by faith. They simply trust God and doubt not and are not bothered by all the ramifications that confuse most people. I would not be dogmatic on this point. I do believe that many people could be healed who are not because they do not pray the prayer of faith. But these "choice spirits" get more things from God than healing. They get guidance and comfort, strength and courage and anything else they need. They simply believe God. They command mountains to move and they move. They pray and then believe they have received what they desired. They ask for wisdom and ask in faith, nothing wavering. They cast all their cares upon the Lord, commit their way unto Him, trust in Him and He brings things to pass. They are careful for nothing but thankful for everything. They do it while the rest of us talk about it, argue about it, measure it by human explanations on one hand and by human experience on the other, instead of saying, "Let God be true but every man a liar."

You can be one of these "choice spirits." The way is clear: a simple, steadfast faith; complete detachment from the world; sincere and unreserved commitment to God. Can you meet that test?

KNOWING WHAT TO DO

> *And of the children of Issachar, which were men that had understanding of the times, to know what Israel ought to do . . .* (I CHRONICLES 12:32).
>
> *And that, knowing the time, that now it is high time to awake out of sleep; for now is our salvation nearer than we believed* (ROMANS 13:11).

THE CHILDREN of Issachar had more than a knowledge of the times: they had an understanding of the times that produced a knowledge of what God's people ought to do. Modern experts have a knowledge of the times. Listen to the news reporters; read the columnists; hear Dr. Toynbee for instance. But they do not understand the times. When men do not know the Scriptures and the power of God, they err, our Lord said. Certainly these men do not know what God's people ought to do today. The most important business we have is to find out which way God is going and get going in that direction. If we are to chart our course correctly, it must be done in the light of several tremendous truths.

First, there is *the promise of our Lord's return*. The church missed the road centuries ago when it stopped looking for the King to come back and began building the kingdom down here. There is indeed a spiritual kingdom, which is not meat and drink but righteousness, peace, and joy in the Holy Spirit, and the reign of God in the hearts of men. The visible kingdom will not be brought in by education, legislation, and reformation, even under religious auspices. It will be set up when the King comes back. If that were understood, misguided souls would not be riding all kinds of queer bandwagons, trying to bring in a counterfeit millennium, and superimposing a false kingdom of heaven—a profane Paradise—on an unregenerate society.

The early church went forth with the proclamation of Christ come, living in the prospect of Christ coming by the power of Christ contemporary . . . *"lo, I am with you . . ."* (MATTHEW 28:20) I believe that we are in the last days. We have had many of the signs of the times before, but not concurrent as in the present pattern.

However, we have more to do than to sit with folded hands, waiting to be rescued by Christ's return. There is a second consideration: *the possibility of a great revival* —a visitation from above, with God coming down in a latter rain of a great awakening. There have been such mighty occurrences in the past when there were nationwide movings of great multitudes, like a wheatfield before a summer wind. We have not seen that in this generation and it is doubtful whether there can be a deep revival among such shallow people. Revival, however, does not have all the answers. Someone has compared such resurgences to a sale in a department store. The sale may be more spectacular, but the main business is done in the daily merchandising the year round. Pentecost was a great day, but the steady growth came as the Lord added to the church daily. Revivals make headlines, but when the books are added up at the last day, it will be found that the main work was done by the faithful preaching of ordinary pastors, the daily witnessing of ordinary Christians, and soul-winning in home and church. We do need revival and while we cannot produce it, we can pray and prepare for it.

If the Lord tarries and revival does not come, there

is the *prospect of retribution*—the judgment of God on unrepentant men. America is a Belshazzar's feast, and that feast was marked by *revelry, revelation* and *retribution*. America is on a national binge, being not yet two hundred years old and dying of moral cancer before our eyes. The decaying carcass awaits the vultures. God has written His warning on the wall and there are few Daniels who will dare to read it. Daniel did not say that he couldn't read it. There are ministers today who cannot read God's handwriting. They do not understand the times nor the meaning of history. Daniel did not read something else. There are false prophets who interpret revelation to mean what God never meant. The Book of Revelation tells us of a final Babylon, ecclesiastical and political: the final amalgamation of collectivized humanity into a world church and world state under antichrist. We need a Daniel who can stand in the midst of this Babylon, turn down the rich fare of Nebuchadnezzar, defy the decrees of Darius, and in the midst of the revelry read the revelation on the wall, predicting retribution to a trembling Belshazzar. The *Interpreter's Bible* to the contrary and notwithstanding, Daniel understood the times and knew what God's people ought to do.

Now, while we await the *return* and pray for *revival* and face *retribution*, is there anything more that Christians can do than just be faithful? Is it the best that we can do just to maintain business as usual? Sometimes we hear church services announced "as usual." Maybe that is what is wrong with them! Nothing else is as usual these days. We need to go on an emergency basis, for the hour is too late and the need too great to go about it as though we had a thousand years in which to complete the job. We have no business living ordinary lives in such extraordinary times.

Against the background of *the promise of our Lord's return, the possibility of revival* and *the prospect of retribution,* we need to project a *program of the remnant.* By that I mean we ought to gather a Master's minority, the faithful few, the company of the committed, a spearhead of expendables, the church within the church. Our Lord stands at the door of Laodicea in these last days and says, ". . . *if any man (anyone) hear my voice and open the door, I will come in . . .*" (REVELATION 3:20). He is calling out the assembly of the anyones!

Dr. Torrey used to say: "In order to have a revival, let a few members of any church get thoroughly right with God." We have been doing things the extensive way in our church life. It is time to start doing things the intensive way. We've been doing it the big way; it is time to start doing it the little way. You will remember that God told Gideon he had too many soldiers in his original army of thirty-two thousand. He had too many of the kind he had for the kind of battle he was out to fight. The church is in spiritual warfare and the weapons of that warfare are not carnal. The average run-of-the-mill church member is untrained and unqualified for this kind of fighting. We have too many of the kind that most of them are, and if we won the battle, we would take the credit for it ourselves, as God told Gideon. We are not going to win this war by a motley mob of the cowards and careless, but by a minority committed in holy desperation—a dedicated few to permeate and infiltrate the world as the salt of the earth.

The faithful minority in our churches cannot get at the unreached multitude outside because of the unfaithful majority on the inside. We cannot reach the goal for stumbling over our own team. We furnish our own interference. We need to rally a Gideon's Band, a bundle of human kindling wood who will instead of letting the majority inside the church and the multitude outside chill their zeal, warm up the church and start a fire in the world as our Lord came to do. This is the strategy of the remnant and the only program that will work today. If it be objected that such procedure would mean two churches in every church, do we not have that situation already: those who are active for Christ and those who by their very inactivity for Him are active against Him? Did He not say, "*. . . he that gathereth not with me scattereth abroad*" (MATTHEW 12:30)?

So, while we wait for the return of our Lord and pray for revival and face retribution, let us rally a remnant with understanding of the times to know what God's people ought to do.

The pastor should lead the way in recruiting the church within the church. There will be problems. Sometimes church policy is in the hands of men and women who know nothing of New Testament standards, and couldn't care less. The pastor must decide whether to bring the flag back to the regiment or try to make the regiment catch up with the flag. The temptation will be strong to accept the status quo and be an ordinary church. Of course, no church is perfect. The New Testament churches were not perfect, but they had a standard and dealt with anyone who tried to lower that standard. Paul did not accept conditions in Corinth as normal. They were subnormal and he would have them normal. We have been content with the subnormal for so long, however, that normal New Testament Christianity appears to most church members to be abnormal!

Of course it goes without saying that this remnant, this church within the church, must not become a little clique of super saints proud of their spiritual superiority. Sometimes these super saints become snooper saints, spying on all who do not dot their "i's" and cross their "t's" to suit them. A nucleus of born-again, Spirit-filled, Bible-believing, Christ-centered, soul-winning disciples is the only answer today. Only these will have understanding of the times and know what to do.

JESUS IS LORD

"For we preach not ourselves, but Christ Jesus the Lord; and ourselves your servants for Jesus' sake." (II CORINTHIANS 4:5)

IF I WERE to ask any Sunday-morning congregation, "Do you believe in the Lordship of Jesus Christ?" I would get an easy reply in the affirmative. But if I were to ask each individual in that congregation, "Is He Lord of all you are and have?" we might have a very disturbing and revealing morning! Any church gathering can sing, "Bring forth the royal diadem and crown Him Lord of all," but not all who are willing to crown Him with their lips will make Him Lord of their lives.

Coleridge speaks of "truths often considered as so true that they lose the power of truth and lie bedridden in the dormitory of the soul." The Lordship of Christ is one of these truths. One writer has said that the word "Lord" is one of the most lifeless words in the Christian vocabulary. Yet Dr. A. T. Robertson said that the Lordship of Christ is the touchstone of our faith, and Dr. G. Campbell Morgan has called it "the central verity of the church."

The Lordship of Christ was the initial confession of the church. ". . . if thou shalt confess with thy mouth the Lord Jesus, and shalt believe in thine heart that God hath raised him from the dead, thou shalt be saved" (RO-

MANS 10:9). When a Jewish convert in the early church said, "Jesus is Lord," he meant that Jesus was God; and when a Gentile believer said, "Jesus is Lord," he meant that Caesar was no longer his god. Polycarp went to his death affirming the Lordship of Christ above the claims of Caesar. In the New Testament it is never "Christ and . . ." because one never needs to add anything to Jesus. He is Alpha and Omega and all the alphabet between. But it is "Christ *or* . . ." the world, Christ *or* Belial, Christ *or* Egypt, Christ *or* Caesar." Early Christianity demanded a clean break with the world, the flesh and the devil. That lasted until Constantine made Christianity fashionable and popular. Pagans flocked into the church lightheartedly bringing their idols and their sins with them, and the church lowered her standards to accommodate the influx. We have never recovered from that mistake. Today, although Caesar is dead, too many church members try to serve two Lords, Caesar and Christ, God and Mammon. Churches are filled with baptized pagans living double lives, fearing the Lord and serving their own gods, drawing nigh to God with their mouths and honoring him with their lips while their hearts are far from Him, calling him Lord, Lord, while they do not what He says. We are not only to worship the Lord on Sunday but to serve Him all week.

The Lordship of Christ is the authentic confession of the Christian. "Wherefore I give you to understand, that no man speaking by the Spirit of God calleth Jesus accursed: and that no man can say that Jesus is the Lord, but by the Holy Ghost" (I CORINTHIANS 12:3). Calling Jesus Lord is the authentic work of the Holy Spirit for the old Adam never bows to the Lordship of Christ. Nowadays we have created an artificial distinction between trusting Christ as Saviour and confessing Him as Lord. We have made two experiences out of it when it is one. So we have a host who have "accepted Christ" in order to miss hell and reach heaven, who seem not at all concerned

about making Him Lord of their lives. Salvation is not
a cafeteria line where we can take the Saviourhood of
Christ and pass up His Lordship, take what we want and
leave the rest. We cannot get saved on the instalment plan,
with fingers crossed and inner reservations, as though one
could take Christ "on approval." To be sure, one may
not understand all that is involved at conversion, but no
man can knowingly and wilfully take Christ as Saviour
and reject Him as Lord, and be saved. Paul told the Philip-
pian jailer, "Believe on the *Lord* Jesus Christ and thou
shalt be saved." He presented all three names of our Lord
as Master, Mediator and Messiah. He would not have the
jailer take Christ as Saviour and think over His Lordship
until some later time.

We have only one option: we can receive the Lord
or reject Him. But once we receive Him, our option ends.
We are then no longer our own but bought with a price.
We belong to Him. He has the first word and the last.
He demands absolute loyalty beyond that of any earthly
dictator but He has a right to do it. "Love so amazing,
so divine, demands my soul, my life, my all." How foolish
to say, "Nobody is going to tell me how much to give,
what to do." We have already been told! We are His
and His Word is final.

I came to Christ as a country boy. I did not understand
all about the plan of salvation. One does not have to
understand it, he has only to stand on it. I do not understand all about electricity but I do not intend sitting around
in the dark until I do! But one thing I did understand
even as a lad: I understood that I was under new manage-
ment. I belonged to Christ and He was Lord.

Here is the key to the sad state of many Christians
and churches. There is a cheap, easy believism that does
not believe and a receivism that does not receive. There
is no real confession of Christ Jesus as Lord. It is signifi-
cant that the word "Saviour" occurs only twenty-four times

in the New Testament, while the word "Lord" is found 433 times.

A Christian is a believer, a disciple and a witness. He should become all three at the same time and be all three all the time. The believers were called disciples before they were called Christians. The Great Commission bids us make *disciples*. God is not out just to save sinners but to make saints out of sinners. The crisis is followed by continuance. "If ye continue in my word, then are ye my disciples indeed." Peter was still a believer but not a disciple after he denied his Lord until after he was reinstated with the "Follow me" of Tiberias. The angel at the sepulchre said, "Go . . . tell his disciples *and Peter. . . .*" The believer comes *to* Christ; then as a disciple he comes *after* Him. Some take a stand for the Lord and keep standing. They take a step but not a walk. I heard a missionary say, "Too many of us are singing, 'Standing on the Promises' but we are really just sitting on the premises!"

The birth of a child is an important event, but it takes twenty years after that to make a man or a woman of that child. Evangelism is thrilling business but it is only the beginning. The believer must be developed as a disciple and witness. On the Damascus road Saul started right: "Who art thou, *Lord? Lord,* what wilt thou have me to do?" He began by confessing Jesus as Lord. Thomas cried, "My *Lord* and my God!" John Wesley tells us that several mornings after Aldersgate he awoke with "Jesus, Master" in his heart and mouth. The Holy Spirit had done His work. Dr. E. Y. Mullins says, "In applying for membership in a Baptist church, faith in Christ *and acceptance of His Lordship* is a prime condition."

Salvation is free. The gift of God is eternal life. It is not cheap for it cost God His Son and the Son His life, but it is free. However, when we become believers we become disciples and that will cost everything we have. Our Lord lost some of His best prospects on this very point. It appears that He lost three in the last six verses of the ninth chapter of Luke. He lost the young ruler. What a prospect he was! He had manners because he came kneeling. He had morals for he had kept the commandments. He had money for he would not let it go. He was a good catch but the Lord did not catch him. When the sick and sinful came to Jesus, He dealt with them in tenderness. But to prospective followers He threw a stern challenge: *"Let the dead bury their dead: but go thou and preach the kingdom of God"* (LUKE 9:60); *"No man, having put his hand to the plow, and looking back, is fit for the kingdom of God"* (LUKE 9:62). To the multitude He gave three "cannots" of discipleship (LUKE 14:25-33). But our Lord was after disciples, not mere "joiners." Americans are notorious joiners. Give them a red button and a certificate and they will join anything. We would have taken the young ruler into church immediately and made him treasurer but our Lord would have him mean business.

The New Testament teaches not only faith in Christ but following Christ. "Come unto me . . ."—that invites the believer. "Learn of me . . ."—that makes the disciple. The Word of God knows nothing of that strange variety of Christian willing to take Christ as Saviour but unwilling to confess Him as Lord. He is not only Saviour of the soul, He is Lord of the life.

The lordship of Christ will be the ultimate confession of creation. We are told that one day every knee shall bow and every tongue confess that Jesus Christ is Lord, to the glory of God the Father (PHILIPPIANS 2:9-11). I do not ask the sinner, "Will you confess Jesus as Lord?" for that he must do now or later. I ask, "When will you confess Him as Lord—now while you can live for Him or beyond the grave when it will be too late?" A flour company had a slogan, "Eventually—Why Not Now?" Eventually every tongue will confess Jesus as Lord, in heaven, on earth, under the earth. But why not now?

Is He your Lord? Is He Lord of your body, your

thoughts, your tongue, your temper, your spare time, your life plans, your pocketbook, your church life, your recreation, what you listen to by radio and look at on television? His Lordship covers everything from eating and drinking to world problems. But it is not bondage, it is freedom, for ". . . where the spirit of *the Lord* is, there is liberty." We are free to do everything that is good and right, in our relationship to God, ourselves and everybody else.

The heart of revival, of the deeper Christian life, of Christianity, is making Jesus Lord. Have you done it?